Single Servings

Single
Servings

Mille Crawford Bell

Drawings by Elsie McCorkell

CROWN PUBLISHERS, INC. / NEW YORK

The section "Dinner Party for One" *first appeared in slightly different form in* Modern Maturity *(February/March 1978), copyright* © *1978.*

Copyright © 1980 by Mille Crawford Bell

Inquiries should be addressed to Crown Publishers, Inc.,
One Park Avenue, New York, New York 10016

Printed in the United States of America

Published simultaneously in Canada by General Publishing Company Limited

Library of Congress Cataloging in Publication Data

Bell, Mille Crawford.
Single servings.

Includes index.
1. Cookery. I. Title.
TX652.B39   1979   641.5'6   79-17154

ISBN: 0-517-538636 (cloth)
        0-517-538644 (paper)

10 9 8 7 6 5 4 3 2 1
First Edition

To the memory of

my MOTHER & DAD

BERYL *and* LOUIS J. CRAWFORD

Contents

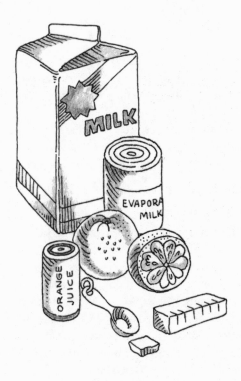

Introduction

This book is for . . .

. . . People who work, live alone, and prepare meals for themselves.

. . . People who are retired, or for some other reason live alone and do not work.

. . . The teenager who must cook for him/herself while his/her parents are away. Unless, of course, he/she runs down to the nearest hamburger stand for dinner.

. . . Women who find themselves alone while husband and kids are off on a camping trip and have trouble adjusting to "something decent to eat" because they've been used to quantity cooking.

. . . Men who find themselves alone while their wives and children have gone to visit Grandma and have been used to having a cook.

. . . Men, once married but now single, who have a hard time knowing *how* to cook, let alone what to cook.

. . . Couples, where one person is on a medical diet and the other one isn't. The other one gets rather tired of eating diet-prescribed dishes. Some of these recipes are for dieters, but only insofar as controlling the cholesterol and sodium intake is concerned.

. . . The young man or woman getting started in his/her first apartment.

. . . And, in general, for anyone who is alone, regardless of age and sex, and who doesn't eat out all the time.

When I was growing up, my sister and I had to help Mother get supper. I especially remember the potatoes. We had a battered kettle, about 14 inches across and 10 or 12 inches deep. We also had a large family. Supper was always started by filling the kettle with potatoes. Vegetables were measured by the kettleful also, though it wasn't the same kettle, unless we were having string beans. We usually had roasts of some kind, and they were always about 10 pounds. There were often instructions when we sat down to dinner. Mother would say, "Now don't think you're going to eat all that meat tonight because, if you do, you won't get any sandwiches for lunch tomorrow. I've marked the spot where you have to stop." And she had. About 4 inches from the end of the roast would be a cut, and the meat from that point to the end would be needed the next day.

Then I got married. Those first few months were torture. I was so used to measuring by the kettleful that when I fixed potatoes for my husband and myself I had to call my mother long distance to find out how many to use. When I looked at those two potatoes, I thought we would starve, and any piece of meat I served looked like it belonged at a child's tea party! Gradually my family expanded, and soon we were all adults—at least as far as eating was concerned. I could cook in quantity again.

Eventually, though, I was alone and had to readjust to the smaller quantities of food preparation. Being alone, the one compensating feature I found was that now I could fix all those interesting dishes I'd been wanting to cook for years. The transition from being part of a large family to being single presented some very different problems, though. Every recipe I looked at served from six to as many as twenty or more people. I had two choices. Either I'd have a diet of the same type of food every day—steak, hamburger, pork or lamb chop, all broiled or fried—or I'd have to use my ingenuity and develop some special recipes for one. You won't find many exotic recipes here, but you will find old standbys with a new twist. The result of all my efforts is this book, geared to one serving.

I compiled the recipes over years of coming home tired and hungry, and having to fix dinner. The problem I've tried to eliminate is spending a great deal of time in the kitchen after a full day's work, while ensuring a variety of meals—some quick, some quicker. There are also recipes for Saturday and Sunday, when one has a little more time to play with.

Food budget has played an important part too. My food budget has never been as large as I'd like to have it, so I've discovered ways of keeping my grocery bill down. The costly part comes when you buy prepared or packaged foods and all those tempting snacks. Frozen dinners are convenient to have on hand, but you can also make your own. My experience with purchased frozen dinners has been that one package is never enough, and in the time it takes to cook one of them, you could have prepared a fresh meal. In terms of money, the meals you make yourself, as opposed to prepared frozen ones, reduce the grocery bill considerably.

Prepared cake mixes have been a boon, with excellent taste and variety. The trouble is, the cake is often too much for one person. Most of the recipes require two eggs, often a cup of milk, and you still must mix it and bake it. Most of the ingredients for a cake may already be on your pantry shelf—shortening, flour, flavorings—and you surely have the eggs and milk. As far as I'm concerned, although cake mixes serve a fine purpose, they are too expensive and are designed for a family serving; usually about half the cake goes to waste. I always think I'm going to eat it all before it dries out, so I don't put it in the freezer, but then I don't eat it after all. As a result, I have to throw away quite a lot of the cake. Maybe this has been a problem for you too. Therefore, I've designed the recipes here for small two-pieces-of-cake cakes. Usually one of these cakes is all I want for quite some time.

People alone usually have many time-consuming chores to do and are often quite limited on food budget, so no matter who you are, you need space-, time-, and laborsaving methods, plus economy. That's what I've tried to provide in this book.

Food budget plays an important part in my cooking, as I'm sure it must in yours. More important in developing this book, however, was the physical condition I was in by the end of the day. Though I have worked all my adult life, even while raising a family, I'm now more tired at the end of the day. There isn't anyone else to do the running. If the phone rings, I have to answer it. If the trash needs taking out, I have to do it. If there's dusting or picking up to be done, I have to do that too, if it's going to be done. And then when I'm through with dinner, I still have to clean up the dishes and pots and pans. So I don't feel like standing too long in the kitchen to prepare a meal. This probably applies to you too. So there are many factors involved in these recipes besides the ingredients.

Almost anything you cook can be adjusted in quantity without too much deviation from the original effect. There are a few recipes in this book that make sizable quantities. These are indicated, and in some instances I have given you the recipe for one serving as well as for the quantity serving. Dishes such as stuffed cabbage I make by the pot, divide the quantity into separate servings, and freeze individual portions for a later meal. This is especially handy for the nights you come home from work too tired and don't feel like cooking. Just take a serving from the freezer and pop it into the oven.

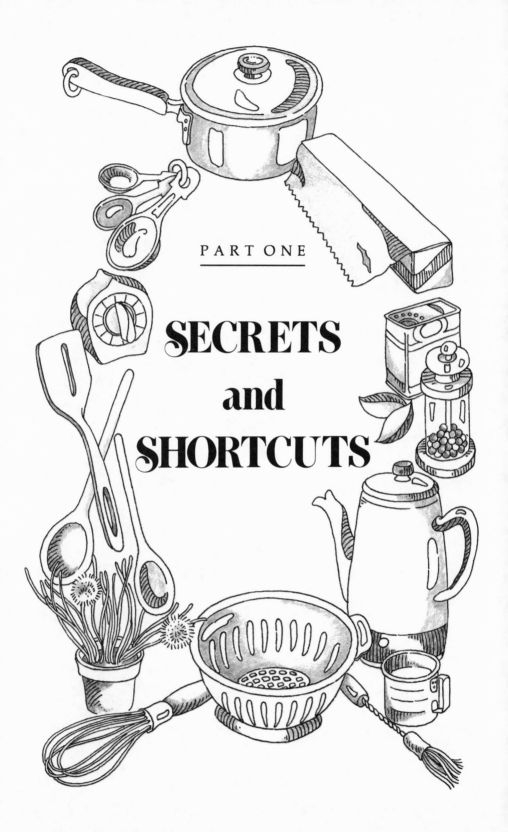

PART ONE

SECRETS
and
SHORTCUTS

1

Stocking Your Kitchen

Whether your kitchen is large or small, whether you cook only for yourself or frequently entertain, your kitchen should be supplied with basic cooking equipment and at least a few herbs, spices, oils, and other condiments, and some staple foods such as potatoes and onions.

ESSENTIAL KITCHEN EQUIPMENT

The amount of kitchen equipment you stock will depend greatly upon whether you cook just for yourself or plan to entertain guests. The following list contains equipment essential to begin preparing meals for yourself, and perhaps one guest. You can gradually add more if you find yourself becoming more involved in cooking.

Two 1-quart saucepans with covers, one stainless steel or enamel for boiling eggs

3-quart saucepan, with cover

5- or 6-quart pan, with cover

10-inch frying pan, with cover

6-inch frying pan, with cover

Small roasting pan with cover

Round or oblong rack to fit roasting pan (for roasting or broiling meat)

2-cup ovenproof casserole, with cover

1-quart ovenproof casserole, with cover

9-inch by 12-inch shallow pan

Small foil pans with covers (for baking or storing)

Set of mixing bowls (three or four bowls), very small to large

Small strainer

Colander

Small coffee maker or teapot or both

Small kettle for boiling water (optional)

Toaster

Eggbeater

2-cup measuring cup

Set of graduated measuring cups (for dry ingredients), $\frac{1}{4}$ to 1 cup

Set of measuring spoons

Set of wooden spoons

Slotted spoon, long handle

Large mixing spoon, long handle

Long-handled 2- or 3-prong fork

Paring knife

Serrated knife (5- or 8-inch blade)

8-inch-long-blade knife

Knife sharpener

Wide-blade spatula (pancake turner)

Long-handled tongs

Pot holders

Vegetable scraper

Grater

Vegetable brush (bristle or plastic)

Can opener (manual or electric)

Combination can punch and bottle opener

Nutcracker

Corkscrew

Several straight-sided small jars with screw tops for storage (you
can collect these gradually as you use up jarred foods)

Several small plastic containers with covers for storage

Canisters or large jars for storing flour, sugar, beans, pasta, and so
on

Used can to hold grease and drippings, for disposal in trash

Foil wrap

Plastic wrap

Plastic bags

Paper towels

Two or three cotton or linen dish towels

Timer

If you plan to do any baking you will need the following:

Three round cake pans

8- or 9-inch-square cake pan

Two 8- or 9-inch pie tins

Two cookie sheets

One or two 6-cup muffin tins

One or two loaf pans for baking bread

Set of rubber spatulas (one wide, one narrow)

Small flour sifter

Eventually, you may want to add some of the "fun" items that soon
will become necessities to you:

Fruit juicer, manual or electric

Metal or wooden mallet for pounding meat

Large wire whisk

Small wire whisk

One or two iced tea spoons

Garlic press

Wok, electric or nonelectric

Electric frying pan

4-quart slow cooker

1-quart slow cooker (preferably with several heat settings)

Hand-held electric beaters
Electric mixer, full size
Blender
Ice crusher
Meat grinder

If you plan to purchase any of the last four items, be sure to look at all brands of equipment; there are many on the market. You should also check out a food processor, which can perform the functions of a mixer, a blender, a meat grinder, and an ice crusher all in one, by means of the attachments. They are more expensive than the individual items, but if your space is limited, as in most small kitchens, you may save both space and money by investing in the do-everything model.

There are many kitchen aids on the market. When you are in the supermarket, a department store, or even a hardware store, look over the many available items. You may find just the little gadget you need to assist you, to make life in the kitchen more interesting and less work and less time-consuming.

ITEMS FOR THE PANTRY

Everyone knows that you need flour, sugar, salt, and pepper in the pantry, but what else do you need to create a variety of meals? Well, herbs, spices, seasonings, and variety vinegars and wines are a few of the secrets that can add interest to ordinary dishes and change a plain meal into something quite delicious.

Part of the fun of cooking is trying new things. For instance, if your recipe calls for cinnamon, you might wonder what would happen if you used nutmeg instead. So, try it. Plain buttered green beans are good, but they take on an entirely different flavor if you sprinkle a little dillseed on them. Or try some mint—or Lemon Pepper, or lemon dill. Or sprinkle tarragon vinegar over them. There is no end to the variety that can be achieved simply by interchanging flavors. Many a new recipe has evolved because one flavoring or spice or herb was not on hand at the time. And because of these numerous ways of changing a simple dish into a creation, you will find that cooking is really fun and not a chore.

When you're getting started in the kitchen, just to furnish the bare essentials can be an expensive proposition. When it comes to spices, herbs, and oils, you could invest a young fortune without realizing it. To help you get started, here is a list of basic seasonings to have on hand. Of course, much depends upon the type of cooking you will be doing. If you aren't going to bake or make puddings, you won't need vanilla or other extracts; so these can be left for a later time.

BASIC SEASONINGS FOR THE PANTRY

Extracts
Vanilla   Almond

Oils
Vegetable oil   Olive oil

Bottled Sauces
Catsup   Worcestershire sauce

Sweeteners
Brown sugar   Honey
Powdered sugar   Molasses

Spices, Herbs, and Seasonings
Basil   Nutmeg, ground
Bay leaves   Onion powder
Bouillon cubes, beef   Oregano
  and chicken   Paprika
Cinnamon, ground   Pepper, black ground
Garlic, powdered   Rosemary
Kitchen Bouquet   Salt
  or other meat extract Tarragon
Marjoram   Thyme
Mustard, prepared, regular,
  or Dijon type

Vinegars

Distilled white or cider   Red wine; flavored or unflavored

Wines

Dry white, such as Chablis   Dry red, such as Burgundy

My spices, herbs, and miscellaneous seasonings have been acquired a few at a time: they make up a long list! I buy everything in jars. One reason for this is that they look nice in a rack on the wall, but the main reason is that I prefer to be able to see immediately how much of any item I have on hand. Also, herbs and spices keep better in glass screw-top jars than in boxes. The air stays out and the flavor stays in until you use the last of the item. Most of the herbs and spices kept in jars will retain their freshness for many months. Some of them I use infrequently, yet they are still as pungent as the first day I brought them home.

I began by keeping my spices and herbs on the wall shelf. It was made to hold the forty-two jars I had at the time, and they were arranged in alphabetical order, rather than in the categories of herbs, spices, and seasonings. I like them in alphabetical order, but that's not the way it is now, for I outgrew the rack. It still has forty-two jars, but there are additional items on double turntables in the cupboard, so they are no longer in alphabetical order. But I find them easily.

In addition, these are what I consider important items for me and normally are always in my pantry:

Extracts

Black walnut   Orange
Brandy   Peppermint
Butter flavor   Raspberry
Lemon   Rum

Oils

Peanut oil   Sesame seed oil

Spices, Herbs, and Seasonings

Allspice, ground   Anise, star or seed

Bell peppers, sweet, dehydrated
Black beans, fermented
Bouquet Garni
Capers
Cardamom, ground
Cayenne pepper (red pepper, powdered)
Celery seed
Chicken seasoning stock base
Chili powder
Cinnamon stick
Cloves, ground and whole
Coriander, powdered
Cream of tartar
Cumin seed, powdered
Curry powder
Dillweed
Ginger, ground and crystallized
Horseradish, bottled
Italian herbs
Lemon dill
Lemon juice

Lemon peel
Lemon Pepper
Meat tenderizer
Mint
Mustard, dry, powdered
Onion flakes
Onion, frozen, chopped
Orange peel, dried
Pepper, whole peppercorns, black and white
Pepper, seasoned
Pickling spices, mixed
Polynesian Luau Seasoner
Poppy seed
Poultry seasoning
Saffron
Sage
Savory, summer
Sesame seed
Seasoned salt
Vanilla bean

Bottled Sauces

Chili sauce
Barbecue sauce
Hoisin sauce
Oyster sauce
Plum sauce

Liquid Smoke
Soy sauce
Tabasco sauce
Taco sauce
Tempura sauce

Sweeteners

Hoisin sauce

Syrup, white corn

Vinegars

Red wine garlic
Red wine eschalot
Red wine tarragon

White wine tarragon
Malt

Wines

Sherry, cooking	Burgundy
Vermouth, dry	Chablis
Sauterne	Marsala
Port	

One word of warning: Don't rush out and buy every item on the list at once! Pick up a few as you need them—some you may never use or want. And feel free to experiment with substitutes. If you don't like oregano (an herb used extensively in Italian cooking), use sweet basil instead. If you have a plain cookie or cake recipe, add one of the other extracts to the batter or dough along with the vanilla. It will change the flavor, and it puts adventure into cooking.

STAPLES AND HOW TO STORE THEM

Every larder, no matter how tiny, should have a few staple foods such as onions, garlic, and potatoes. Storing these in a small kitchen is sometimes a problem, but I have found two solutions. One is to put them into a tray that is raised from the floor of a cupboard so air can circulate around the tray (and its contents). The other way is to keep them in the open, but in a cool place. If potatoes or onions are stored in a dark warm place, they sprout faster than when stored in a cool area. Some people prefer to keep them in the crisper section of the refrigerator. Do not attempt to freeze raw potatoes or onions. They will become unpalatable and almost useless even for cooking.

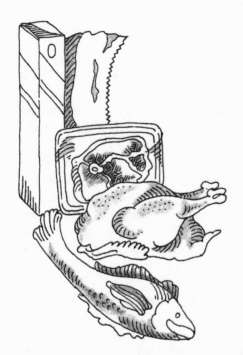

2

The Freezer – and What to Fill It With

I believe that the single person should have a sizable freezer. Not necessarily a huge one, but one with fair-sized capacity—the kind that is at the top of a standard-size refrigerator, preferably with a separate door, and has room for more than just the ice-cube tray. Have you ever noticed that when meat is on sale it usually is sold in large pieces? The smaller the cut, the higher the price. One friend asked me, "What am I going to do with three pounds of round steak, even if it *is* on sale? When I want steak, I'll buy it." If you have a freezer, the answer to this is obvious. When steak or other freezable foods go on sale, you can buy several pounds. Cook one portion the same day; cut the rest into several one-serving portions, wrap well, and freeze for later use. Be sure to mark the frozen portions with the name of the food and the date.

For easy identification, I place all separate servings of any one kind of meat into one large plastic bag. When I want a lamb chop, I have to look only for one bag of lamb instead of moving several small packages and reading all the labels. With all the same kind of meat in one plastic bag, it requires only a glance to know whether you have enough to make that company dinner Sunday or whether you should think about something else. I've planned many a dinner party simply on what meat was in the largest supply in the freezer.

When round steak goes on sale, I buy about a two- or three-pound steak. From one piece I prepare beef Stroganoff or other stew, and then I freeze the rest. Round steak is a versatile meat that can also be used instead of veal in dishes like veal Parmesan, scallopini, or even Weiner Schnitzel, when sliced very thin and pounded. I can have several meals from a three-pound steak for about 30 cents less per pound than it would cost to buy individual portions as I needed them. And look at the trips to the store it saves! Because of the freezer, I am able to shop about once every three weeks—sometimes even less often. This saves time and energy—and money too.

When meat is on sale, I buy enough meat for several servings. I also usually buy a variety of meats—fish, seafood, chicken, beef, pork, lamb, and veal. Remember, a whole chicken may be almost 10 cents per pound cheaper than a cut-up chicken. For the extra savings, I learned how to disjoint a chicken very quickly. I usually buy two or three whole chickens at a time, wrap the pieces individually (or perhaps include one company-sized dinner) in foil or plastic, and put it all in the freezer. If you like to fish, the freezer is an ideal place to store your catch—providing you've caught more than one serving! Also, bread is often on sale, and can be frozen.

The freezer is also useful for storing extra ice cubes if you are having a party. As your trays freeze, just pop them into plastic bags or large ice cube holder, and make more. It's far better and more economical than running down to the liquor store to buy them.

When wrapping for the freezer, make sure that all the air is out of the package and that it is sealed tightly so the moisture will not escape. You can buy special freezer wrap for this purpose, or you can wrap each piece tightly in plastic wrap or foil. After wrapping each piece, place all the pieces in a plastic bag, draw the edges together, insert a straw, and draw out all the air. Then quickly tie the top with a piece of wire. Always label each bag with the name of the food and the date you packaged it.

Certain fresh vegetables may be frozen with good results. When bell peppers are on the market at an inexpensive price, I buy pounds of them, put them in a plastic bag, and keep them in the freezer. Once peppers are frozen, however, they lose their crispness and can only be used for cooking. When they are semi-thawed, I cut off the stems and slice the peppers into whatever shape is needed.

One problem single people have with commercially frozen vegetables is that most packages serve more than one (except those that contain squash and spinach—they're just one good serving for me). For the manufacturer to package these into smaller portions would increase his price, and therefore increase our price, so that leaves us to make our own arrangements.

I put the packages into the freezer as soon as I bring them home from the store, but when I decide that I want peas for dinner, I take out the quantity I want and divide the remainder of the box into small jars, such as baby food jars. One package of peas will make about four $\frac{1}{2}$-cup servings, so I fill three small jars with the remainder of the peas in the package, screw the tops onto the jars, and put the jars into the freezer. Do not thaw the peas (or any other frozen vegetable) when you repackage them. Just whack the package hard on the countertop until the pieces have jarred themselves loose, and then you can put them into the jars and get them back into the freezer before they thaw. Cut green beans can go into these little jars too, but things like asparagus stalks or Brussels sprouts require a taller or larger container. The next time you want peas or asparagus stalks, just twist off the lid of the jar, and presto!—no waste—and only one trip to the freezer.

I have found that opening one end of a frozen food package, pouring out what I want, folding the package back together, and replacing it in the freezer just *isn't* a good idea. Quicker? Yes. But air gets into the package and the food dries out. If I'm not using the small jars method, I always put the box into a plastic bag (so I can still read the label) and put a twist wire around the top. But then you must make two trips to the freezer and go through all that motion at dinnertime, just when you're most in a hurry. I like the jars better because not only are they less work in the long run, but you can tell at a glance just how much you have, and you have saved yourself several steps and several minutes—or seconds—which all add up to energy saved!

Recommended Storage Periods for Frozen Foods

Food types	*Approximate storage periods at 0° F. (months)*
Fruits, vegetables	10–12
Beef, veal	10–12
Lamb, poultry, rabbits, game birds, eggs	8–10
Butter, cheese	6–8
Ground meat (unsalted), fresh pork, ham, lean fish, cottage cheese, poultry giblets	4–6
Beef liver, fatty fish, slab bacon, most cooked foods, baked products, pies—baked and unbaked	2–4
Sliced bacon, leftover cooked foods, unbaked products with yeast, ice cream	up to 1

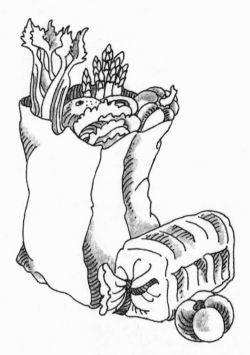

3

Shopping Economically— or the $1.50 Loaf

When my family still lived at home, my big problem with bread was keeping it in supply. Now my problem is keeping it fresh. Even a small loaf is too much to keep unfrozen. I calculated the high cost of bread for the single person at more than $1.50 a loaf, if you throw away three-quarters because it has dried out or molded before you can use it. I doubt that bread was that high even in the Gold Rush days! Now I divide the loaf into two- or three-day portions or however much I think I will eat before it dries out. Then I store these portions in plastic bags in the freezer. When frozen, bread does not take long to defrost. You can pop it right into the toaster, or allow it to thaw naturally as you fix a sandwich.

Also, using this method, you can buy the "giant economy size" loaf and save money instead of buying the higher priced smaller loaf. This same formula applies to other food items as well. I do this regular-ly with meat and frozen vegetables, especially when these items are on sale.

THE TRUTH ABOUT SUPERMARKETS

Four words about "discount" grocery stores (supermarkets): they "ain't" necessarily so. Although supermarket prices are often lower than those of small independent stores, the opposite is sometimes true. Therefore, before you begin to regard your local supermarket as a budgeter's utopia, you'd better know your prices. I do not propose that you run all over town to purchase items at lower prices. That merely uses up time, energy, and gasoline, and is not worth the few extra pennies saved. But if you have occasion to stop off at a neighborhood store—on the way home from work, say—take note of the prices on major items you ordinarily purchase. You may well find them a penny or two cheaper.

However, even though some items may be a penny or two more, there is one major advantage to the small independent store: it can help you cut down your shopping time considerably. There is usually little or no waiting in line to get checked out, especially at the peak shopping hours of four to six in the afternoon, and this can save you as much as half an hour over the typical supermarket.

I still consider my time valuable—and more so, my physical stamina. Consequently, I am willing to pay a penny or two more per item for a half-dozen items in order to spend much less time at the store. Obviously, each of us must make our own decision on this subject.

The small store has other advantages too. The meat you buy there is often of better quality than that sold at supermarkets—it has more meat to the bone, and it's more properly aged and far more flavorful. So it's obviously a commendable buy, despite the few extra cents it costs.

I do not wish to imply that *none* of the items offered in discount supermarkets are worth buying. There are frequently good buys. And some of them are priced at a moderate savings over the prices featured in the smaller stores. The important thing is this: be sure to compare the discounted price against the quality and quantity of the item—or the sacrifice of same—if you wish to gain true value from your shopping and cooking dollar.

One way to determine which market or supermarket to patronize is to keep a record for a few months of what you have bought and how much you have spent at the different stores. You will soon find that one will stand out above the others in value. Keep little notes along with the prices regarding quality, service, and other factors. Not only will you determine which store is best for you, you will also have a good idea of what your store budget is. And remember, a store budget is far different from a grocery budget. Store budgets usually include paper products, grooming aids, household-care items, light bulbs, and sometimes even plants—numerous items that will never find their way into your cooking.

THE PRICE PER POUND DOESN'T COUNT

Take a trip to the butcher's counter in a typical large, modern, well-stocked supermarket. There are so many cuts and types of meat to choose from, you may become confused before you get a good start. It takes one trip down the counter to see all there is, and another trip back to decide what you want and can afford to buy.

Once you know what you want, you have to decide what you can afford. Some people make the mistake of judging meat by the price per pound and therefore are defeated before they start.

Learn instead to look only at the price per package. Then look at the quantity in that package. Is there enough for just one meal? Or will it supply two or three meals? Take seafood, for example—those nice, fresh jumbo shrimp you see in the case. The price per pound may seem astronomical, and you may be inclined to heave a sigh, clench your teeth, and move on, resigned to enjoying shrimp only in your dreams. But stop a minute and think. How many jumbo shrimp would you need for a meal—three, maybe four? And how many are there in the package (which likely weighs less than a pound)—ten, maybe a dozen? That means, if you ate three shrimp for dinner, your entree would cost you one-third of the package price—which likely is only one-sixth of the price per pound. And there is no waste, except for the thin shell.

In comparison, consider that T-bone steak you had last night. The price per pound was fairly reasonable, even if the steak was a bit thin. Of course, there was a good-sized bone to throw away, and you couldn't ease your conscience by giving the bone to the dog because you don't have a dog. Nor did you eat the ribbon of fat around the edge of the steak. By the time you threw away the bone and the fat, both of which figured in the cost per pound for that steak, you probably consumed about 5 or 6 ounces of meat—but you paid for about 9 or 10 ounces. Divide the purchase price by the number of ounces you actually ate, and you'll see that the price per ounce consumed is considerably higher than that shown on the package. That's a good example of poor economy.

You will soon learn that being alone you can eat certain expensive cuts of meat that seem out of reach when you have a family. For example, consider filet mignon. Assume you are looking at a package that has three good-sized pieces of filet in it—thick meat, no bone, and only a tiny bit of fat. Now divide the price by the number of pieces you will need for a meal—usually one piece of filet is sufficient. You'll find that the cost per individual serving is far less than that for T-bone steak even though the cost per pound may be more. This same rule of thumb applies to spareribs and any other cut of meat that can be divided into single servings.

And that is how you can eat better on nearly the same amount of money that you've been spending for dull, unexciting meals. There is no need to restrict yourself to an endless succession of meals made from the same old ground beef (which when cooked loses a lot of fat and ends up half the size you started with and with very little flavor). I am not saying that I eat filet every night—or shrimp either. Quite often I settle for a couple of hot dogs with mustard and lots of onions on a heated bun. I also have things like spaghetti, macaroni and cheese, spareribs, T-bone or rib steak, ground sirloin or ground round, and chicken or chicken livers. But variety I *do* have, and I eat pretty well. My monthly spending at the supermarket is surprisingly low, and that includes buying nonfood items such as detergent, light bulbs, sundries, and sometimes a bottle of wine. And, I might add, I am not a skimpy eater. When I say dinner, I mean a plateful—and my plates are large!

But I will say this: I do not eat a lot of extras. I never buy potato chips or soft drinks, and very little candy, cookies, or cake. Nonetheless, I eat well—and eat what I want. And that makes all the difference.

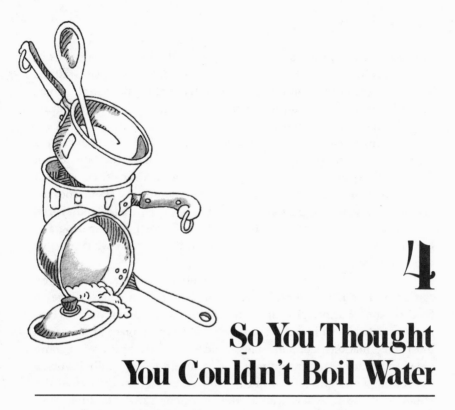

4

So You Thought You Couldn't Boil Water

In the minds of some people women have an instinct for cooking. It's easy to see where that supposedly "natural" instinct came from. When most women were children, they were indoctrinated into the "mysteries of the kitchen" by helping mother scrub potatoes, set the table, and do the thousand other tasks surrounding preparing a meal. Meanwhile, little boys were left to ride their bikes, mow the lawn, and play with their trains. In the minds of earlier generations boys were not *supposed* to be kitchen-oriented—that was woman's work. (Somehow, from this restrictive environment emerged some of the world's greatest chefs—mostly men!)

Besides the chefs, there are thousands of men the world over who are excellent cooks—either by "natural instinct" or simply inclination. How did they learn? The same way women learned. If they were lucky, they had mothers or fathers who were good cooks and who had the interest in teaching them when they were young. Some did not learn until they were grown up, picking up the basics from wives or girl friends, or going back to ask their mothers. Some are self-taught. They love good food, and they've found that making it yourself can be as much a creative enterprise as painting a picture or building furniture and a lot more quickly rewarding!

Any man can learn to cook if he wants to. If you do not have a close relative nearby to turn to for direction, don't hesitate to ask friends or acquaintances for advice—someone in your office, male or female, or your social group. Most people love to talk about cooking and especially love to pass along the "tricks of the trade" and special recipes they themselves have developed. You won't be preparing any gourmet banquets at first, but then you probably won't want to—just good satisfying food.

Once you've got the basics well in hand, there are many ways you can expand your repertory. Most newspapers have a daily or weekly food column that offers recipes and often also shopping tips, such as news on what fresh foods are in season. The family magazines, sold in most supermarkets, contain many articles on food preparation, both plain and fancy. And should you find yourself getting really involved in cooking, you'll probably want to look at some of the magazines devoted solely to food—as well as the enormous variety of cookbooks available in any library or bookstore. (Remember that most cooks rarely prepare a dish that is completely original; at some point they consult a recipe. The difference is in how they adapt it.)

Don't be afraid to start. Cooking is really a relatively simple process for almost all the foods we eat. Everything we eat can be prepared very simply or can be given a new "dress" by the addition of an herb or two or by replacing one or two items of a recipe with something similar, yet a little different.

The biggest bugaboo in cooking for the novice—whether man or woman—is fear. (That isn't mine—mine is cleaning up afterwards!) But fear of the unknown or unfamiliar plays too big a part in the lives of all of us. It is so easy to change that around and think of the unknown as a chance to broaden our education, as an adventure, an experiment, or an exciting experience.

Granted, there is a certain mystery to cooking, but it's intriguing to explore these mysteries. We may never know how baking powder came about or who had the courage to eat the first of anything. It is common knowledge to stay away from mushrooms you find growing in fields and woods unless you are an expert on which mushrooms are edible and which are poisonous. Have you ever wondered about the courage it must have taken for that first person to try a mushroom or a green bean or a carrot? And what about the wonderful imagination of the person who first thought about cooking a carrot, and the later ones who improvised on that first method?

That's the way to approach life in the kitchen—with wonderment and amazement that we are so bountifully blessed with a wide variety of fruits, vegetables, and meats. We could eat for months and never have to have the same dish twice!

As you become more adept in and familiar with the kitchen, you will try more complicated dishes. When you do, you will find that "complicated" is reduced to usually meaning, besides a longer list of ingredients, more bowls, utensils, and several steps in mixing items together—each in its own process, still relatively simple.

CAUTION IN THE KITCHEN

As I said earlier, cooking is nothing to be afraid of—there isn't one piece of food that's going to bite, hit, or scold you. However, there are some things in the kitchen that call for caution. The following are some simple safety precautions to keep in mind when cooking.

- Take care with boiling water and hot grease.
- When heating oil or butter in a skillet, use a low flame—a high flame will cause the grease to sputter and possibly burn you or catch fire.
- Keep your knives well sharpened (you can buy a sharpener in any good housewares shop); a dull knife can slip and cut your finger.
- Be sure to read and follow the directions that accompany your cookware and small appliances.
- Keep all handles of pots and pans turned toward the sides or back of the stove. When a handle sticks out over the front edge of the stove, it's easy to bump into it and flip it over, spilling hot food or liquid. Such a mishap can cause severe burns, not to mention an unnecessary mess on your floor.
- Never reach up to a cupboard above the stove while a burner is

lit. It is very easy for a shirttail or sleeve to dangle over the flame and catch fire.

• Don't stretch to reach for a basket or plate on the top shelf—use a stool or stepladder instead. It's not only easier that way, but it will prevent you from dropping something because you weren't able to get a good grasp on it.

• Do not keep any cleaning agent (liquid or powder) in the cupboard where you keep food. That way there's no chance of confusing a bottle of salad oil with a bottle of liquid detergent! Be especially careful to store poisonous items separate from foods.

• Keep all cupboard doors closed when not in use—not to keep the kitchen looking nice, but to avoid bumping into them. If you are bending down to get something from a lower cabinet, be sure the top cupboard doors are closed *before* you stoop down. That way you'll avoid bumping your head when you stand up again.

• If you have rugs in the kitchen, be sure they are firmly anchored. Flimsy rugs are dangerous anywhere, but especially in the kitchen.

• If you spill or drop something, pick it up and clean the floor immediately. The few minutes you spend now will prevent you from slipping and falling later on.

• Most kitchens are equipped with many electrical appliances, and most of these are safe to use if you first use some common sense. Never, never touch anything electrical if your hands are wet or if you have spilled liquid on the floor and are standing in it. Water is a conductor of electricity and the combination of the two can cause a severe shock. You cannot be too cautious in this area.

 Metal is also an electrical conductor. Never insert a fork or knife into a toaster that is in use. If you must dislodge a piece of toast that's stuck, be sure to unplug the toaster first.

• Washing dishes also calls for caution. If you wash dishes in a sinkful of bubbly water, be very careful. Never put glasses, glass dishes, or knives (even table knives) in the water along with other dishes. Glasses can easily break, and a piece of broken glass or the blade of a knife picked up inadvertently while it is submerged in the water can cause some terrible cuts on fingers and hands. Set these items aside, and wash and rinse each one separately before putting it in the drainer.

- Hot pans from the oven can cause severe burns. If you are going to leave a hot pan of baked food sitting on a counter for a while, it's a good idea to drape a pot holder over the edge of the pan. You may leave the room for a moment and attempt to pick up the pan when you return, forgetting that it is hot. The draped pot holder will remind you not to touch the pan.
- Keep your pot holders handy while cooking. Storing them in a drawer is nice, but not practical. It's a good idea to use a pot holder or tongs to remove a baked potato from the oven. And if you cook with a cast-iron skillet, be sure to grasp the handle with a pot holder. The handle gets almost as hot as the bottom of the pan.
- Do not keep flammable decorations, such as cute baskets, decorative pot holders, or curtains, over the stove. If you ever have a small fire from the bottom of a pan, or in a pan, the flames could easily ignite these items and cause the fire to spread in a hurry.
- If the grease in a pan or the stove catches fire, do not throw water on it; that will simply cause the grease, and the fire, to spread. Keep a container of baking soda within easy reach of the stove and use it to douse a grease fire. Flour thrown on burning grease is also effective.
- Never put your bare hand in the garbage disposal in your sink. This might seem unnecessary to mention, but I have known two grown women who have experienced near disasters with their garbage disposals. One was stuffing garbage into the disposal with her bare hand, when her hand slipped and plunged through the opening. Fortunately, she closed her fist and pulled her hand out in time so it was not cut severely. The other woman was trying to clean out a clogged disposal, using her bare hand, without first turning off the machine. As she cleared it out, the machine began working rapidly. Fortunately, she only nicked her finger on the bone that she had removed. She could have lost several fingers. It's best to use a wooden spoon, a broom handle, or such to push food through the opening or to retrieve an item that has accidentally slipped into the disposal. (It's quite easy for a piece of silverware to slide down, especially when the sink is filled with water and dishes, and it's always a good idea to check before turning on the machine. Be sure to turn off the machine *before* you attempt to put anything into it.

- If you have a microwave oven, it is important to check the seal on the door, especially if you've had your oven for a long time. To check for escaping radiation around the door (which you should do at least once a year), contact the office of the Food and Drug Administration in your area. This agency will test the level of radiation your oven emits at no charge.

I have not told you these things to frighten you. On the contrary, if you use simple common sense and good judgment, and work in the kitchen only when you are alert and aware of things, you won't run into trouble.

5

About Timesavers, Shortcuts, and Substitutions

For most of the cooking I do, there are no hard, fast rules about any of the dishes—*except* when it comes to baking a cake, which must be done with precision. Generally I always look for the *easy* way. That's because basically I'm a lazy person. But I accomplish much more than a lot of energetic people I know.

One friend of mine keeps a little quote on her desk in constant view. It says, "Reduce everything to its most simple form." Though it was meant for use in writing letters, it holds a great lesson for almost any application. For example, observe how many times you walk between the stove and the utensil drawer for forks or spoons, or how many times you go to the cupboard to take out the individual ingredients for a cake. Could you have taken two or three items out at once? Or perhaps your kitchen cabinets and drawers need rearranging.

We are all creatures of habit, of course. And sometimes a habit is carried over from childhood because it is the way our mother did something. Look around your kitchen. In a few minutes you can probably think of at least three ways to alter things that will reduce your kitchen work-time by hours.

Single people have more demands on their time than do others because they have no one to share the chores. To save your time, try to plan your shopping ahead. Keep a list in the kitchen, and as you begin to use up an item, put it on the list. When it's time to go to the store, you will know—without having to check the refrigerator and pantry—just what items you need. And if you have the space, keep a "reserve" of items on hand. When you take a reserve item for use, put the item on your shopping list. That way, you'll never run out of often-used items. This system (along with my freezer) enables me to go to the store only every two or three weeks—and sometimes even less often. I always have food in the house—enough in fact so that if the need arose, it would last about two months without requiring a trip to the store. It wouldn't be very glamorous eating, of course, and it might even get downright monotonous, but at least it would be food.

Yet even I have to admit that occasionally I look into the refrigerator (whose back wall I can't even see) or open each of the four compartments of the freezer (whose back walls I also can't see) or prowl through the pantry shelves laden with jars of rice, spaghetti, macaroni, and noodles, as well as canned goods (which are never in great abundance), and complain to myself, "Nothing to eat!" It happens to all of us occasionally. That's when the precooked and frozen dishes come in handy.

COOKING PACKETS: THE SIMPLE WAY TO DO IT

We don't want to spend all our time in the kitchen washing up pots and pans. Besides, doesn't that ½ or ¼ cup of peas rolling around on the bottom of a quart pan look rather silly?

Instead of having three or four pans on the stove, I have done much of my cooking in one pan by making foil pouches and fitting them into the pan. Into each foil pouch I place one item—for instance, sliced carrots, peas, leftover mashed potatoes. And in a flatter packet that I place (gently) over the top of these pouches I put a slice of roast or other leftover meat, if I have it. Add ⅛ to ¼ cup of water to the pan, being careful not to get it into the pouches. Bring the water to a simmer, cover the pan with a tight-fitting lid, reduce the flame, and let the food heat for about twenty minutes.

You can cook fresh vegetables this same way, but you must remember to use vegetables that require about the same length of cooking time. I have prepared as many as five items for one meal this way, using only one pan.

The quantity of packets you put into the pan depends on the size of pan you use. A 1-quart pan holds two packets, a 2-quart will hold from two to four packets, depending on what you put in each. Empty the packets onto your plate, and rinse out the pan—no washing needed! I usually use the heavy-duty foil for this, although I have used regular-weight foil many times. You can leave about a ¼-inch to ½-inch opening at the top of the packet, or you can pinch the edges together until they are touching, but do not twist them together because that will make the packet too difficult to open.

When you cook this way, you are doing yourself several favors at once. Not only are you saving on labor (washing dishes and pans afterward), but you are saving on gas or electricity. You are also providing a bigger variety on your plate, and as a result it looks and tastes better, and you enjoy it more. But there's one big factor you don't see, especially if you cook fresh or frozen vegetables: your food is more nutritious. Food cooked in packets is cooked in its own natural juices, which preserves the vitamins and minerals; in fact, some of them will cook back into the food. Finally, your vegetables will retain much of their natural color, crispness, and texture, and will be tastier to eat.

One word of caution, however. Do not salt the vegetables until after they are cooked. Cooking by the steaming method puts the natural salts back into the vegetables, so that if you salt them while they are cooking, you may find they are too salty. So taste them after cooking and then add salt, if you must. Most people salt vegetables simply to replace the flavor cooked out of them when they were boiled in quantities of water. With packet cooking, that is not a problem.

If you like your vegetables "buttered," add butter or margarine to the pouch when you put the vegetables in.

ABOUT SLICING VEGETABLES

People spend too much time and effort on simple tasks such as slicing vegetables. Typically, they hold the carrot or celery stalk in one hand and the knife in the other, then they slice—one slice at a time. If you were cooking two carrots a person for six people, this would require a lot of individual cuts. Why not try a simpler method, even when you're cooking for one? Place the carrots side by side on your cutting board; align the tips evenly by butting the blade of the knife against them. In this way, you can slice two—or more—at one time. You may need ten strokes to cut the carrots, but that's quicker and easier than ten strokes times two carrots and you've just reduced your total labor by 50 percent. And that's not to mention the time you've saved.

If I can reduce the time or motion spent by at least one-half, I feel well satisfied. Later, I'll work on the remaining 50 percent and see if I can reduce it by half again. Meanwhile, when you have the carrots all sliced on your cutting board, simply use the knife blade to slide the pieces into the pan. This also applies to string beans, celery, onions, or anything else you cut into small slices.

There's a trick to slicing an onion easily and efficiently. First peel it, then cut off a thin slice on one side, so that the onion will not roll. Holding the root end with your other hand, cut from the tip to the root, without slicing off the slice. Stop just short of the root. When all slices have been made, cut across the root end and the slices will fall off, quickly and easily.

To dice an onion, peel it, then cut a thin slice off the root end so that the onion will stand flat. Make parallel slices down from the top to the root, but not through the root. Turn the onion, making a series of slices perpendicular to the first. Space the slices $\frac{1}{8}$ to $\frac{1}{4}$ inch apart. When this is done, turn the onion on its side and slice through the cuts at $\frac{1}{8}$- to $\frac{1}{4}$-inch intervals and the diced onion will automatically fall away. If you want only a little diced onion, make the same type of slices, but cut down only about $\frac{3}{4}$ inch.

A word about knives. If you have a chef's knife, learn to use it. It's a very versatile instrument, though it does take practice. A chef's knife—sometimes referred to as a French chef's knife—is about $14\frac{1}{2}$ inches from tip of blade to the end of the handle. The blade is a modified triangular shape, much longer than wide. To use, grasp the blade near the handle with your forefinger and thumb, with your thumb and forefinger resting against the handle. With the other hand, grasp the top edge of the blade at the tip end with the thumb and forefinger. Do this firmly. To chop, hold the tip end in one place and gradually move the blade with the other hand, up and down and from side to side. As the food spreads out, use the knife blade to push the food back to the center, and continue chopping. It will be quite clumsy in the beginning, but with practice you will soon get the hang of it and become quite proficient.

When you can use the chef's knife properly, you needn't even move the knife tip to chop vegetables to whatever size segments you desire. You can also use your chef's knife for mincing such foods as parsley and cabbage. And to help make your work easier, good, old-fashioned carbon steel knives—though not as pretty as stainless steel cutlery—are the best tools available. They do turn dark and have to be scoured once in a while, and they have to be sharpened, though less often than knives of the stainless steel variety. But they hold a very sharp edge, and because their blades are thinner than those of stainless steel, they cut much easier and faster.

ABOUT SUBSTITUTIONS

Often a recipe calls for an ingredient that is really rather commonplace such as orange juice or wine, but because we don't happen to have that particular ingredient on hand, we skip over the recipe entirely. Also, as we peruse cookbooks, we often see recipes to "Serve Six," when, in fact, we wish only to make something special for ourselves.

Measurements in many recipes are merely guides that can be varied to suit your taste. Also, sometimes you may not even need to use the ingredients called for. Let your imagination roam. Not only is this how new and novel recipes are born, but it also enables you to achieve variety and flair in your menu. Naturally, if a recipe calls for grated coconut, you probably aren't going to substitute grated ginger. But if a recipe calls for cinnamon, you could easily substitute a little nutmeg, allspice, or cloves. Also, if you are baking a cake or making a cheese soufflé, you need to follow the measurements precisely. But if you're mixing up a casserole or stew, be creative about using foods you like or happen to have on hand—even if the recipe doesn't suggest it.

Perhaps you have noticed that some recipes use the word "optional" after an ingredient. This means that if you happen to like that item, or have it on hand, use it—but if you don't like it or don't have it on hand, the recipe will still turn out well.

Another phrase often used is "taste and correct the seasoning." Many people think this refers to salt. Not true. There are other seasonings besides salt. For example, there's the tangy sharpness of vinegar, the richness of molasses, the sweetness of sugar or honey. Sometimes the only thing the dish needs to achieve that mellow or subtle taste is to blend in the pot for a fairly long time. A dash—a mere dash—of garlic powder does far more for a recipe than salt. I often use a tiny speck of garlic powder in mashed potatoes and leave out the salt. In boiling potatoes I sprinkle a little garlic powder in the water instead of salt. It gives a new dimension to the flavor. In the majority of recipes that call for butter, I use unsalted margarine instead—because I'm one of those on a "medical diet." When milk is called for, I use either low-fat or canned evaporated skim milk, which I mix with a can of water. These substitutions do not change the flavor of the recipe, though they *do* make it more "healthful"—lower in fat and salt. They are also a great boon in reducing cooking costs.

Some recipes call for chicken broth, beef bouillon, or stock as the cooking liquid. But suppose you don't have any? But why not just use a bouillon cube or the granulated bouillon now available in stores? Simply dissolve the needed amount of cubes or granules in water. In fact, at times I simply sprinkle a crumbled bouillon cube into the mixture and then add the water. The only thing you must pay attention to is how strong a flavor is desired. Normally, you would use one bouillon cube to 1 cup of water. However, I prefer *two* cubes to 1 cup of water. It's a matter of personal taste.

SOME ADDITIONAL HINTS

To keep bean sprouts fresh: Rinse them, then place in a container (such as a plastic bowl with an airtight cover). Cover them with cold water, then cover the container. Force out all the air by lifting an edge of the cover while pressing down in the center of the cover. You'll hear the air rush out. Change the water each day, or every two or three days. Bean sprouts will keep fresh this way in the refrigerator for three to four weeks. Simply take out the quantity you need, drain, and use. At the same time drain off and replace the storage water, then return the container to the refrigerator.

To obtain half an egg: One egg (large AA) contains about 2 tablespoons of egg white and 3 teaspoons of egg yolk. To obtain half an egg, break the egg, separate the egg white into a plastic container and the egg yolk into a small container the size of a sauce dish. Both should have covers. Next, prick the membrane of the egg yolk until the yolk spreads. Using an appropriate-size spoon, measure out the amount of yolk you need. Use this same procedure to measure out the amount of egg white you need.

Egg whites and yolks stay fresh a long time if kept in covered containers in the refrigerator. Be sure to use airtight containers, however. Otherwise, the yolk will dry up in three to four days. Whites will last a bit longer.

To substitute for chocolate: If you're out of chocolate or are not supposed to eat it because of the cholesterol, you can achieve the same taste and results by using 3 tablespoons of cocoa and $1\frac{1}{2}$ teaspoons of vegetable oil. In a cake, for example, simply add the cocoa and oil to your recipe—there's no melting needed.

Butter substitutes: Many recipes in this book call for butter, but the majority were made with unsalted margarine. While butter, in some instances, will produce a richer flavor, in some of the recipes, such as the one for Rich Crispy Cookies, there is no discernible difference in taste using margarine. If you want to reduce your cooking costs, margarine is an excellent substitute: it can be used interchangeably in all recipes that call for "shortening" as well. I use unsalted margarine exclusively.

Milk substitutes: When a recipe calls for milk, you can substitute canned evaporated milk, either the regular or the skimmed variety. Just mix it in a jar with an equal amount of tap water. If you purchase the small-size cans, you can always be sure of having fresh milk for cooking. That way, you can use your homogenized milk for drinking. While this canned milk substitute does not perform as effectively as the fresh in recipes such as tapioca pudding, it is excellent in most other dishes, particularly baked and creamed items. Where regular canned milk is called for, however, as in Old-Fashioned Potato Soup, this diluted milk does not work well. To obtain the richness, use whole canned milk as suggested. You can also substitute powdered milk in many recipes.

Flour substitutes: Cornstarch or arrowroot may be used instead of flour as thickening agents for gravy. For every 2 tablespoons flour, use 1 tablespoon cornstarch or $\frac{1}{2}$ to 1 tablespoon arrowroot. Note that the results of these three substances are not the same. Flour makes an opaque sauce, while cornstarch and arrowroot make a translucent sauce. Arrowroot requires low-temperature cooking and is not recommended for brown gravies.

To obtain $\frac{1}{8}$ or $\frac{1}{4}$ pound (2 to 4 ounces) of boneless meat: Use a pork chop, veal chop, lamb chop, or small steak. Chop, slice, mince, or cube the meat as required. If "ground" meat is called for, chop the meat very fine and add sufficient water so that the meat is of a moist consistency. If your recipe calls for bite-sized pieces of pork, buy pork riblets and slice the meat between the ribs. These are lower in cost than spareribs and equally tasty.

Miscellaneous suggestions:

- To add interest to vegetables, cook them in chicken or beef broth instead of plain water. Make the broth by putting the required amount of water in a saucepan, then crumbling in half a bouillon cube. Serve the broth with the vegetables or save for making a sauce. Cooking in broth adds flavor and pizzazz to an otherwise ordinary-tasting vegetable.

- Bake your vegetables instead of boiling them. If you're having a baked potato, try putting some green beans in a small casserole, add a bit of butter, cover the dish tightly, and bake for about a half hour.

- Most fresh vegetables, such as carrots or zucchini, do not need peeling. Clean them by washing under running water and scrubbing them with a soapless metal or plastic pad or scrub brush. Most of the vitamins and minerals are contained in the skin and should be retained in cooking.

- Paprika is rich in potassium. Use it lavishly as a colorful garnish on vegetables, mashed potatoes, and meat or fish dishes.

- If you are going to quick-fry vegetables, as for a stir-fry recipe, dry them on paper towels after washing them. They won't splatter as much in the oil as when they're still moist from washing. Pat-dry sliced potatoes before frying for the same reason.

6

The Spice of Life

COOKING WITH WINE

Since I've lived alone, my food seems to require a bit more zip to whet my appetite. If you find that true as well, why not try cooking with wine? It does wonders for bringing out the flavors of food and adding a "little something" to an otherwise plain dish. Many people have told me that they have wanted to try cooking with wine, but they thought it would be expensive, or require gourmet expertise. Not true. You can begin cooking with wine today. And in most cases, for mere pennies per meal.

There are many wines on the market, both imported and domestic. They come in many sizes, from the little tenth- or half-bottles to full gallons. But you won't need a gallon, and you won't need to use the costly imported wines. California and New York wines are excellent. Besides, the majority of people are *not* wine connoisseurs—certainly not me. If you buy a large bottle of wine and have some left over, just keep it tightly corked and store it so that the cork stays moist. You can use it again and again. After two or three weeks it may turn slightly sour, but it will still be fine for cooking and add an interesting flavor. If you are planning on drinking some of it, you can also store it in the refrigerator to keep it from turning.

In single-serving cooking, you will rarely use more than a quarter cup of wine in any one recipe—and often only a tablespoon or two—so by purchasing the small sizes of wine you can have wine on hand to cook with—and even drink—without bending your budget out of shape. The small bottles of wine that are sold in the grocery section of your market are only for cooking: they rarely make good drinking wine. They are relatively inexpensive, and one bottle will last you a long time. Many types of wine are available this way—reds, whites, and sherries among them.

One word of caution: I recently bought a couple of bottles of cooking wine at the market without reading the label carefully. Several days later, I discovered that it was "seasoned"—blended with several ingredients that would not have worked well in my recipe. Be sure to read the label when you buy wines, and for greater flexibility choose only the unseasoned ones—those that contain no added ingredients such as salt, sugar, or spices.

You'll find a vast number of uses for wine in cooking, such as in stews, spaghetti and other sauces, vegetable-meat soups, and in many Chinese and French dishes—a lot of American ones too.

Don't overlook those little bottles of wine you often see near the cash register in a liquor store. They're usually about five inches high, cost less than a dollar, and offer quite a bit of variety: dry vermouth, for instance, which can be used in any recipe that calls for dry white wine; sherry; flavored wines such as plum, apple, and grape; and even sake and other specialty wines.

A few drops of wine can perk up the simplest meat or fish dish. You, too, can cook with flair with the simple use of spices, herbs, wines, flavored vinegars, and other ingredients. There's no great secret in knowing how. Just open a bottle of wine or assemble different spices, use what you need, and—presto!—your meals take on a whole new excitement! You'll probably find a lot of adventure right in your kitchen.

DINNER PARTY FOR ONE

Eating alone can be delightful—if you make it so.

Come evening, we trot to the kitchen and prepare dinner. Nothing special—whatever's easiest. Then what do we do? We sit in the same place, with the same dishes, looking at the same things every day—the same surroundings, the same television program, the newspaper, or a book. The whole procedure lacks inspiration, enthusiasm.

Are we letting ourselves get too far removed from making dinner an occasion? For the most part, I think so.

May I suggest that at least once a week you treat yourself to a special dinner-party atmosphere? Set the table. Put a lighted candle on it and add a vase of flowers. Turn on some soft music. Have a goblet of wine. Dim the lights a little in the dining area.

Make your solo dinner a delightful experience, with as little distraction as possible, in pleasant surroundings, with attractive objects to look at. Don't do anything else while you eat—don't read, don't watch television, don't write letters. Just have dinner in your special setting—relax and enjoy the atmosphere.

Instead of a mere necessity, dinner will become a pleasant experience. The soft candle glow will relax you. Even a paper napkin will take on an air of sophistication and your stainless flatware will feel better. If you have silver flatware, use it. There's no reason to keep it stored away in that silver chest under the bed. Put some in the kitchen to use every day.

Keep a couple of nice glasses in the kitchen too. If you don't have crystal, buy a piece or two, or at least some good-quality stemware. And forget the "utility" angle. A good piece of glassware will probably outlive the old jelly glass anyway, and it certainly provides more pleasure.

With candlelight and silver, and wine in your goblet, your old dishes will look better. And dinner will taste better.

Another way of combating the monotony of eating alone is to change table settings. Be extravagant—in ideas, if not in money. What you eat *from* is as important as what you eat. If you don't like your present dishes, or if you're tired of eating from the same ones all the time, how can you expect to enjoy even the fanciest gourmet meal you might prepare?

Being single, you don't have to buy a complete service for four or more. Most dishes are available in individual place settings—one dinner plate, cup, saucer, dessert or bread-and-butter plate, sauce dish, soup or salad bowl. Buy one; then, as your finances permit and your mood urges, buy another.

Give yourself variety. Pick different colors, shapes, and designs. Bright yellow will automatically cheer the grayest day. And don't be confined by tradition or habit. There are designs and colors to fit any mood. For fall, a dinner of pork chops, mashed potatoes, and bright green peas would be delightful on a brown-and-white plate, with a brown napkin and wooden-handled flatware. A table set with a blue place mat, blue gingham dishes, silverware or pastel blue-handled flatware, a blue goblet, and a small floral arrangement would be perfect for a summer meal on the patio or porch or next to an open window.

Today's dishes come in many shapes. Round plates still predominate, but you can also choose from dishes that are octagonal, hexagonal, square, and oval. Today's colors, too, are as bright as a box of new crayons: solids, two-tones, plaids, geometrics, freeform patterns, traditional flowers, and mixtures in colorful, wild profusion. The range of hues is remarkable and refreshing.

Maybe you'd like something old and delicate. Try antique shops, flea markets, swap meets, garage sales. You'll often find exquisite pieces costing little. It's not necessary—or even desirable—that everything match. Take a tip from the Chinese: their rice bowls rarely match anything else on the table, yet all are eye-appealing. This applies to the rest of us, as well. Potato soup, for example *tastes* better from a formal maroon and gold-bordered soup plate than when served in plain white.

Single place settings of flatware are available in nearly all patterns, from elegant sterling to casual service with handles of wood, bamboo, or bright-colored plastic.

Place mats and tablecloths are offered in almost anything you could want. You can find them in all sorts of fabrics—including laces—that are machine washable and dryable and need no ironing. Or, if you sew, tat, or crochet, you can make your own, with several napkins to match or contrast.

These niceties help quell the defeat we feel when we allow ourselves to get into a rut with dinnertime. Too often, the single person thinks, "Why bother—no one here but me." But it's vital to your well-being that you not allow yourself such a rut.

Move around. If you're a couch-sitter, move to a chair. Or out to the patio, or in front of the fireplace. If you've been eating in the kitchen, move to the dining or living room.

Arrange your plate, as well as your eating area, to please your eye and your mood. Plan courses that take time to eat (soup, salad, a fresh artichoke) so that you won't rush through your meal and be finished almost before you've begun.

Don't nibble during the day: you want to save your appetite for dinner. And work out an interesting meal, putting as much enthusiasm into it as you would for guests. Enthusiasm is always the first step to enjoyment. Tape a sign to your refrigerator or cupboard door that reads, "Plan something new for dinner!" You'll find yourself trying new foods, preparing familiar ones in new ways, and hunting for special dishes in which to serve them. You'll look forward to your special dinner party for yourself, you'll plan to do it more often, and your life will become more exuberant.

In short, treat yourself to a special dinner party at least once a week. Indoors or out, new dishes or old, the change will aid your digestion and pick up your spirits. You'll soon find yourself eagerly anticipating the next one—and you'll feel much more the whole person you really are.

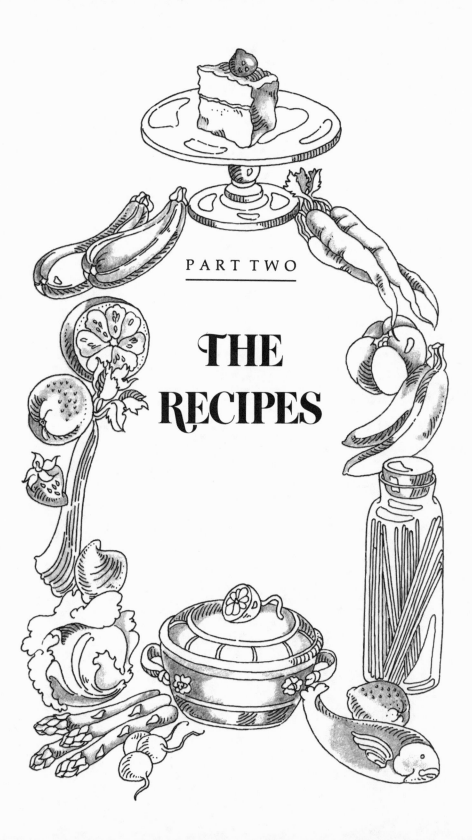

PART TWO

THE
RECIPES

7

A Few Simple Breakfasts

Sliced Peaches with Strawberries

1 medium-sized fresh peach
A few fresh strawberries
2 teaspoons sugar (approximately)
Heavy cream, half-and-half, or milk (optional)

Run hot water over peach to help loosen the skin. Then peel peach, cut in half, and remove pit. Slice peach into a bowl. Clean strawberries, and, depending upon size, slice berries over cut peaches. Sprinkle with sugar. Serve with cream, if desired.

This is a dish that is better when made ahead. Toss the fruit and sugar, and store covered for a few hours. Sugar will draw through fruit and provide more juice.

A dish of fruit and a slice of toast is a refreshing, light breakfast during any season, but especially in summer when fruit is more plentiful.

Hot Chocolate

1 ounce (square) unsweetened chocolate
2 teaspoons sugar
1 teaspoon butter or margarine
1 cup milk
$\frac{1}{3}$ to $\frac{1}{2}$ cup miniature marshmallows (optional)
Dash of salt
$\frac{1}{2}$ teaspoon vanilla extract

Grate the chocolate into a 1-quart saucepan. Add the sugar and butter and heat over a low flame until the chocolate melts; stir to a smooth paste. Add a little milk (about 1 tablespoonful) and stir until smooth, then add a little more milk and blend again. Simmer this for a few minutes to cook the chocolate, stirring all the time. Slowly pour in the rest of the milk, stirring continuously, and add half the marshmallows. Heat until the marshmallows nearly dissolve and the milk is hot.

Remove from the heat and add the salt and vanilla extract, stir to mix well. Taste for sweetness; if you add more sugar, stir to dissolve. Put the remaining marshmallows into your cup and pour the hot chocolate over them. Serve. Marshmallow cream may be substituted for the marshmallows.

Low-Cholesterol Hot Chocolate

3 tablespoons cocoa
$1\frac{1}{2}$ teaspoons vegetable oil
2 teaspoons sugar
1 teaspoon margarine
1 cup low-fat milk
Dash of salt (optional)
$\frac{1}{3}$ to $\frac{1}{2}$ cup miniature marshmallows
$\frac{1}{2}$ teaspoon vanilla extract

Mix the cocoa and oil; add the sugar and margarine and blend well. Add about 1 tablespoon milk and stir until smooth, then add about $\frac{1}{4}$ cup milk and mix again. Cook over a low flame to blend the flavors, about 3 minutes, then slowly pour in the rest of the milk, stirring all the time. Add the salt, if desired. When the chocolate is hot, drop in about half the marshmallows and let them dissolve. Remove from flame, add the vanilla extract, and stir. Taste for sweetness. You might wish to add more sugar; if you do, stir well to dissolve. Put the remaining marshmallows into your cup and pour the hot chocolate over them. Marshmallow cream may be substituted for the marshmallows.

This is a rich, satisfying snack, yet has a low cholesterol content for those who are on low-cholesterol diets and tastes the same as regular hot chocolate.

Egg Nog

1 egg
1 teaspoon sugar
½ teaspoon vanilla extract
1 glass milk
Dash of nutmeg or cinnamon (optional)

Break an egg into a small bowl. Beat with a wire whisk until foamy and liquefied. Add the sugar and vanilla extract; stir to dissolve. Pour into a tall glass. Add milk and stir to combine milk and egg. Top with nutmeg or cinnamon, if desired.

This can also be made in a blender by adding all ingredients to the blender; whip a moment and pour into a glass. Sprinkle with nutmeg or cinnamon.

Banana Shake

This makes an excellent quick breakfast.

1 ripe banana
1 egg
1 cup milk, approximately
$\frac{1}{4}$ teaspoon vanilla extract

Place the banana in a bowl and mash with a fork; then add egg and beat with an eggbeater till smooth. Or place banana and egg in a blender and blend until liquefied. Add milk and vanilla extract and beat or blend a few more seconds. Pour into a glass and serve.

Variation: Other fruits can be used, such as oranges (peeled, with the white membrane removed, and seeded), peaches or apricots (both skinned and with the pit removed), strawberries, or any other fresh fruit you may desire. You can also combine fruits for a variety of flavors.

Eggs Goldenrod

2 eggs, hard-boiled
$\frac{1}{2}$ cup medium white sauce (see p. 168)
Salt and pepper to taste
1 or 2 slices toast
Paprika to taste

Chop egg whites; reserve yolks. Add the egg whites to the white sauce. Heat thoroughly, add salt and pepper, and pour onto toast. Sprinkle with egg yolks rubbed through a sieve. Sprinkle paprika over the top. Serve.

Cheese Omelet

2 or 3 eggs
Salt and pepper to taste

Oil, butter, or margarine for cooking omelet
¼ to ½ cup grated Cheddar cheese

Break eggs into a bowl and beat until light colored and foamy. Add salt and pepper.

Heat oil, butter, or margarine in an 8-inch skillet. When pan is hot, pour in beaten eggs and, over moderate to low flame, allow eggs to set and puff up. If you wish to hurry it up, you may run a spatula around the edges of the pan, gently lifting the cooked portion up slightly, tilting the pan and allowing the uncooked portion to drain down around the sides of the pan. When top is well set, sprinkle the cheese over the top. Mark the top across half of the omelet and, with a spatula, fold one side of the omelet over onto the other side and slip out onto plate. Serve hot.

Variation: Other foods may be added to the omelet, such as diced green pepper, minced onion, chopped ham, sausage, or crumbled bacon.

Pan-Scrambled Eggs

1 or 2 eggs
1 teaspoon water (optional)
1 teaspoon butter or margarine
Salt and pepper to taste

Break eggs into a bowl. Beat with a fork until well blended. Add a little water if desired, and beat into the eggs.

Heat butter in skillet over medium heat. When butter is bubbly, pour in eggs. Allow them to set a few moments. As they begin to turn color, stir eggs with a fork, slightly if you prefer large "curds," or thoroughly if you prefer a creamy consistency. Add salt and pepper and stir to blend. Remove to plate. Serve.

Variations: Bits of precooked sausage, ham, or crumbled bacon may be added to scrambled eggs if you desire. Or try a pinch of chopped parsley or dill. Add them while eggs are beginning to set, and stir them into the eggs as the eggs cook.

Sweet Milk Pancakes

¾ cup biscuit mix, unsifted
1 egg
1 tablespoon vegetable oil
Milk

Measure biscuit mix into a bowl. Break egg into a measuring cup and add the oil and enough milk to reach the ½ cup mark. Beat this together, then stir into the biscuit mix, stirring just enough to blend well. Do *not* beat out all the lumps.

Lightly grease a griddle or frying pan and heat to medium on stove. If using an electric pan, set the temperature accordingly (about 380° F.). Pour in batter to the size pancake you desire. Bake on one side until lightly browned, then turn and bake the other side. Tiny bubbles will form—the more bubbles, the more thoroughly the pancake is cooked. Do not pat down the cooked side after you turn the pancake because that will toughen it.

If you prefer thick pancakes, add a bit more biscuit mix or use less milk. This recipe makes about 4 pancakes, approximately 5 inches in diameter and ½ inch thick.

Buttermilk Pancakes

6 tablespoons flour
¼ teaspoon baking soda
1 teaspoon sugar
1 egg
1 tablespoon vegetable oil
6 tablespoons buttermilk

Mix flour, baking soda, and sugar in a bowl or a large (2-cup) measuring cup. In a 1-cup measuring cup, mix the egg, vegetable oil, and buttermilk. Pour the liquid into the dry ingredients, and stir until blended.

Pour the batter directly from the measuring cup onto a lightly greased hot griddle (380° F. electric frying pan) to form 3 to 4 pancakes. Tiny bubbles will form on each pancake. When each is covered with bubbles, turn and brown the other side. Do not pat down the pancake after turning it.

Makes 3 pancakes about 5 inches in diameter and ⅜ inch thick.

French Toast

1 egg
2 tablespoons flour
2 teaspoons water
Salt to taste (optional)
Nutmeg *or* cinnamon to taste (optional)
2 slices white or sourdough French bread, preferably day-old
Oil for frying (about ⅛ to ¼ inch deep in skillet)
Garnishes: jam, jelly, syrup, confectioners' sugar, as desired

Break egg into a wide shallow dish such as a soup plate or pie tin. Beat with a wire whisk until foamy. Add the flour and stir into egg. Add the water and stir until smooth. Add salt and spice if desired, and stir well. Heat the oil in a skillet.

Cut 2 slices of bread in half on the diagonal. (They will fit into the pan better this way.) Dip each piece of bread into the egg mixture, coating both sides and all edges. Allow bread to soak for a few minutes, then remove with a fork, allowing excess to drip off. Carefully slide the bread into the hot oil. Fry until golden brown on one side, then turn and brown the other side. Drain on absorbent paper. Serve with jam or jelly, or syrup, or dust with powdered sugar, as desired.

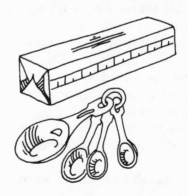

California French Toast

1 egg
1 tablespoon milk
2 tablespoons flour
⅛ teaspoon cinnamon
⅛ teaspoon nutmeg
⅛ teaspoon ginger
Oil for frying
2 to 3 slices of bread (preferably day-old)
Garnishes: butter, syrup, confectioners' sugar, jam, as desired

Beat the egg and milk until light and fluffy; add the flour, and beat until smooth. Add the spices and stir well. Heat oil in skillet until very hot. (Use a deep-fryer if you have one.)

Dip the slices of bread into the batter, coating them evenly on all sides, and then carefully slide them into the oil. Fry until golden brown on both sides, then drain on absorbent paper. Do not crowd the pieces of toast in the oil.

Serve with butter and syrup or powdered sugar or jam.

If you cut the bread on the diagonal, you will find that the pieces will fit into the pan better. Leave some room around each slice to allow for bubbling.

Sherried French Toast

2 slices day-old bread *or* fresh bread set out for ½ hour to air-dry
1¼ tablespoons sugar
¼ cup pale dry sherry or white wine
1 egg
½ teaspoon powdered ginger
¼ teaspoon ground cinnamon
Salt and pepper to taste
Oil for frying
Garnishes: butter, syrup, confectioners' sugar, as desired

Cut the bread slices in half on the diagonal.

Dissolve the sugar in the wine and soak the bread in the wine-sugar mixture a few minutes.

Beat the egg until foamy. Add the ginger, cinnamon, and salt and pepper.

Heat the oil in a skillet, and when hot remove the bread from the wine-sugar mixture and dip into the egg mixture. Slide the egg-coated slices into the hot oil and fry until lightly browned on one side; turn and fry the other side.

Drain on absorbent paper, then serve with butter and syrup or powdered sugar.

Milk Toast

Milk Toast is good for a late-night snack, especially when you are not feeling well or are too tired to cook.

1 cup milk
1 teaspoon sugar
Salt and pepper to taste
1 teaspoon butter or margarine
2 slices bread

Mix the milk with the sugar, salt, and pepper. Add butter and heat in a saucepan over a low flame. While it is heating, toast the bread. Place toast in a soup plate or bowl, pour the hot seasoned milk over it, and serve.

8

Soups

Mushroom Soup

2 or 3 dried imported mushrooms, soaked in cold water for about ½
   hour or until clean
½ tablespoon uncooked rice
1½ cups cold water
¾ teaspoon beef or chicken soup base
1½ tablespoons butter or margarine
1 small carrot, minced
¼ teaspoon celery seed *or* 2 tablespoons minced celery
1 small onion, minced, *or* 2 tablespoons minced onion
¾ teaspoon flour
Worcestershire sauce to taste
Tabasco sauce to taste
Salt and pepper to taste

After the mushrooms have been cleaned, cook them in water in a saucepan for about 20 minutes, until tender. Drain and chop fine—there should be about 2 tablespoons.

In a large saucepan, cook the rice in the 1½ cups of water until done, about 15 to 20 minutes. Add the beef or chicken soup base. (You could cook the rice in chicken or beef stock if you'd like.)

Melt about half the butter in a skillet and sauté the carrots, celery, and onion until tender but not browned. Mix the remaining butter with the flour to form a paste and add the paste to the soup; stir until smooth. Add the mushrooms and the sautéed vegetables to the soup, stirring constantly. Season with a few drops of Worcestershire, Tabasco, and salt and pepper. Simmer for about 15 minutes, stirring frequently, then serve.

Variations: If you like a smooth soup, puree it in a blender before serving. If the soup is too thick, add a bit more water or stock to achieve the consistency you'd like, but correct the seasoning if you add more water.

Oyster Stew

1 cup milk
1 8-ounce can small oysters
½ teaspoon butter or margarine
Salt and pepper to taste
Dash of cayenne pepper, if desired

Pour milk into a 1-quart saucepan. Open the can of oysters and drain the liquid into the milk. Heat the milk and, when hot, add the butter and oysters. Continue heating until edges of oysters curl and oysters are hot through. Add remaining seasonings, stir, and serve.

French Onion Soup with Croutons

1 tablespoon butter or margarine
½ tablespoon vegetable oil
1 onion, thinly sliced or diced
Dash of salt
½ to 1 tablespoon flour
1 can (10½ ounces) beef bouillon and ½ can water *or* 2 beef bouillon
   cubes and 1¼ cups water
Salt and pepper to taste
Croutons (recipe follows)
Grated Romano or Parmesan cheese to taste (optional)

In a 1-quart saucepan over moderate heat, blend the butter and the oil. Stir in the onion and salt, and cook, uncovered, over low heat, stirring occasionally, for 10 to 20 minutes, until the onions are a deep golden brown. Sprinkle the flour over the onions and stir until all the flour is moistened. Cook, stirring, for 2 to 3 minutes. Remove from the heat, and add the bouillon and water. (If you use bouillon cubes, dissolve them in the water or crush them, sprinkle over the onions and stir well, then add the water.) Return the soup to low heat and simmer, partially covered, for 20 to 30 minutes, until well heated and the onions are tender. Taste for seasoning, adding salt and pepper if needed. Prepare the croutons while the soup is cooking.

Pour the soup into a bowl, sprinkle in the croutons, and shake grated cheese, if desired, over the top.

If you prefer not to make croutons, brown a slice of sourdough French bread in the toaster, place the toasted slice at the bottom of a soup plate, pour the soup over it, and add as much cheese as you like.

Croutons

Olive oil to cover the bottom of a small skillet
1 clove garlic, crushed, *or* ¼ teaspoon garlic powder
1 to 2 slices sourdough French bread, cut into ¾-inch squares

In a small, heavy skillet, heat the oil almost to the smoking point. Add the garlic, and stir well, over moderate heat. Add the bread squares and, stirring constantly over a low fire, brown them to a golden color, turning them over and over to brown evenly on all sides. Remove from heat and drain on absorbent paper.

Old-Fashioned Potato Soup

1 large russet potato
1 medium-sized Spanish onion
Water
1 small can (5.33 ounces) evaporated milk
1 to 2 tablespoons butter or margarine
Salt and pepper to taste

Peel and dice the potato and the onion. Place the pieces in a 2-quart pan. Add enough water to just barely reach the top of them, but do not cover them with water. Bring to a boil, and, as soon as the water begins to simmer around the edge of the pan, lower heat so they will simmer. Cover the pan with a tight-fitting lid. (If you don't have one, keep a watchful eye on the water level in the pan: it's important for the success of your soup.) Cook for about 20 minutes.

When the potatoes and onions are very tender, remove the pan from the heat, and, using a fork, mash about half of the potatoes and onions by pressing them against the sides of the pan. Add the milk, butter, and salt and pepper. Return the pan to low heat and continue cooking just until the soup begins to simmer. Taste for seasoning, and correct if necessary.

Delicious anytime. In fact, if you're a working person, why not make a double recipe and take a thermos to work with you tomorrow? It makes a wonderful, inexpensive lunch.

Split Pea Soup

1 cup green split peas, washed
1 quart water
$\frac{1}{2}$ to 1 teaspoon onion powder
$\frac{1}{2}$ teaspoon garlic powder
$\frac{1}{2}$ beef bouillon cube
Pinch of cayenne red pepper

Place all ingredients in a 2-quart saucepan and mix well. Cook, uncovered, over medium heat at a slow boil until soup thickens and peas are tender—about 45 minutes. Put the soup through a sieve, using a wooden spoon to mash the peas through the sides of the sieve (or mash them with a fork right in the pan). If you prefer a puree, put the soup in a blender set at puree speed and blend for a few seconds. Return the soup to the pan, taste and correct the seasoning if needed, and reheat if necessary. If soup is too thick, thin with a little water, but be sure to recheck the seasoning if you do. Serve hot.

Makes two bowls of soup. If you have some left over, put in airtight container and freeze. If you wish to carry some in a thermos for lunch at work, be sure it is quite thin. Split pea soup thickens heavily if allowed to stand overnight. To dilute, just put soup in pan, add about 2 tablespoons water, and stir. As the soup heats, it will thin down. If necessary, add a bit more water for desired consistency. When hot, pour into widemouth thermos bottle, recap, pack a spoon, and take for lunch.

9

Salads and Salad Dressings

Green Salad

Salad adds not only texture and color to a meal, but also minerals, vitamins, and roughage—all necessary to good health.

A salad can be almost anything—and almost any variation on anything. The basis for most salads is greens. These can be lettuce, spinach, endive, romaine, butter lettuce, escarole, chicory, or any other tender leaf vegetables. The simplest salad is iceberg lettuce torn into small pieces served with a salad dressing. Another version is a mixture of two or more greens, prepared the same way. Bits of raw or cooked vegetables, sliced or chopped hard-boiled egg, or bits of thinly sliced meat can be added to the greens.

An easy way to make a mixed green salad is to use two or three types of greens. After washing the leaves in a bowl of cold water and drying them, tear them into small pieces and put in a plastic bag. Store in the refrigerator. (They will stay fresh for several days.) As you prepare meals just reach into the bag and take out as much as you will need. However, be careful in your shopping to buy small heads of greens. When they are torn into bits, they make a huge bagful, and unless you like a lot of salad often, you will find you might have more than you can use.

To help keep your torn greens fresh longer, line the plastic bag with damp paper toweling. The moisture will help maintain the freshness longer.

Avocado Half

½ avocado, pit removed
1 lettuce leaf (or shredded lettuce)
French dressing

Place the avocado half on the lettuce leaf or shredded lettuce. Pour French dressing into the cavity. Serve.

Variations: Fill the cavity with diced cooked chicken, tuna chunks, or small shrimp before adding the dressing.

Note: To store the remaining avocado half, do not remove the pit. Cover avocado with plastic wrap or foil or place in a plastic bag or airtight container. Store in refrigerator.

Cabbage-Carrot Salad

1 thick slice cabbage
1 carrot
Raisins
Salad dressing or mayonnaise to taste

Finely chop a slice of raw cabbage. Grate the carrot on the fine blade of the grater. Add a few raisins, toss to mix, and add salad dressing or mayonnaise. Serve.

Chef's Salad

A Chef's Salad can be composed of almost any combination of vegetables, meat, and cheese of your choice. The following is a guide to help you get started. Because of the variety of ingredients, use only a small amount of each one.

1 cup (approximately) shredded lettuce or other greens
2 tablespoons of any of the following, or combination of the following: cooked or raw grated carrot, cooked peas, cooked green beans, thin-sliced raw turnip, cooked beets, drained
1 small tomato, cut into pieces, or 2 or 3 cherry tomatoes, halved
1 small slice ham, cut into thin strips
1 egg, hard-boiled, cut into slices
1 piece Swiss cheese, cut into thin strips
Salad dressing

Put lettuce into salad bowl, add any vegetables you choose, add the tomato pieces, ham strips, and egg slices. Toss, if desired. Top with cheese strips. Pour over this any salad dressing of your choice, home-prepared or bottled. Serve cold.

Variations: Use Cheddar or any other cheese instead of Swiss cheese. Use salami or any other meat in place of ham.

Caesar Salad

A meal in itself. Serve as the main dish for a refreshing lunch or light supper.

⅓ cup fresh or packaged croutons (see recipe p. 172)
⅓ head romaine lettuce
1 teaspoon dry mustard
1 teaspoon black pepper
¼ teaspoon salt
3 tablespoons Parmesan cheese
1 tablespoon olive oil
Juice of ⅓ lemon
2 anchovies, chopped (optional)
1 small egg

Prepare croutons. Wash romaine leaves, pat dry, then tear into bite-sized pieces into salad bowl. Sprinkle dry mustard over leaves. Then sprinkle in the black pepper, salt, and Parmesan cheese. Add the olive oil and lemon juice by dribbling over top of leaves. Add the anchovies. Break the egg into the greens and toss gently, till well mixed. Do not toss too vigorously or leaves will be bruised. They should be well coated, and no excess liquid should remain in the bottom of the bowl. Taste for seasoning, then add the croutons. Serve immediately.

Cucumber Salad with Sesame Seed Oil Dressing

½ medium cucumber
¼ teaspoon soy sauce
1 teaspoon white vinegar
¼ teaspoon sugar
½ teaspoon sesame seed oil
Dash of Tabasco sauce, or a few grains of cayenne red pepper
Dash of salt

Peel the cucumber and cut it in half lengthwise. Scoop out the seeds, then cut the cucumber into ¼-inch slices.

In a small bowl, combine the soy sauce, vinegar, sugar, oil, Tabasco or cayenne, and salt. Stir well. Add the cucumber, and toss well to coat each slice with the dressing. Chill slightly and serve.

The sesame seed oil gives a delectably nutty yet subtle flavor to this unusual dressing.

Cucumber in Sour Cream

$\frac{1}{2}$ large cucumber
$\frac{1}{4}$ cup sour cream
1 teaspoon sugar, or to taste
1 teaspoon cider vinegar, or to taste
Salt and pepper to taste

Wash cucumber, slice into very thin slices, and place in salad dish. In a cup or small bowl, mix the sour cream, sugar, and cider vinegar; add salt and pepper. Taste, and adjust sugar or vinegar as you desire. Pour over cucumber slices. Serve cold.

Fruit and Cottage Cheese Salad

Fruit and Cottage Cheese Salad can be made from any fruit that has a large pit in it, such as peach, avocado, and pear, or a deseeded tomato. It can be served alone or on a bed of lettuce.

2 leaves lettuce
$\frac{1}{2}$ peach, pear (either canned or fresh), avocado, or 1 whole tomato, deseeded
1 tablespoon cottage cheese, or enough to fill the cavity
Sour cream, mayonnaise, or salad dressing

Shred lettuce, if you are using lettuce, onto a salad plate. Place fruit or tomato on lettuce. Fill cavity with cottage cheese. Add a dab of sour cream, mayonnaise, or other salad dressing. Serve.

Note: To deseed a tomato, cut a slice off the top and scoop out the seeded area with a spoon. Discard the seeds.

If you are using canned peach or pear halves, drain them thoroughly before using.

Fruit Salad

¼ cup diced apple
¼ banana, sliced
¼ cup diced orange
¼ cup pineapple pieces
¼ cup yogurt or sour cream
1 tablespoon (approximately) pineapple or orange juice

Place diced fruit in a bowl. Mix fruit juice and yogurt until well blended. Pour over fruit and toss. Serve.

Spinach Salad

Spinach, in the amount you wish
Olive oil
Lemon juice to taste
Garlic powder to taste
Salt and pepper to taste
Parmesan cheese, grated, amount as desired

This is one of those recipes that you play around with. You can make it as "cheesy," "lemony," or "oily" as you wish.

Wash spinach well and pick out any discolored leaves. Tear into bite-sized pieces and put in salad bowl. Dribble olive oil over the pieces, then do the same with the lemon juice. Sprinkle on a wee bit of garlic powder, salt, and freshly ground black pepper. Top heavily with grated Parmesan cheese. Toss well to coat leaves. Serve.

Variation: If desired, you may add any or all of the following: 2 to 4 fresh mushrooms, sliced; all or part of a hard-boiled egg, sliced, chopped, or put through a sieve; 1 to 2 strips of bacon, cooked and crumbled.

Spring Salad

¼ head lettuce
1 small tomato cut into eighths
2 radishes, sliced thin
1 or 2 green onions, sliced thin
¼ cucumber, sliced thin

Wash and dry the lettuce, then tear into bite-sized pieces. Add the tomato wedges, radish slices, green onion, and cucumber slices. Add your
favorite salad dressing and toss. Serve cold.

Waldorf Salad

Waldorf Salad is an old standby and a great favorite because it is so
simple.

¼ cup diced celery
¼ cup diced apple
1 tablespoon chopped walnuts or pecans
Mayonnaise

Mix the diced celery and apple and add the nutmeats. Use just enough
mayonnaise to moisten the mixture. Serve chilled. If you wish, you
may also add a few raisins.

Watercress and Water Chestnut Salad

½ bunch watercress
boiling water
2 fresh water chestnuts, peeled, *or* 2 canned water chestnuts, drained
¼ teaspoon soy sauce
½ teaspoon sesame seed oil
Dash of salt
¼ teaspoon sugar

Trim off the ends of the watercress stems, and wash the watercress under cold running water. Then, drop it into boiling water for a second or two, remove, drain, and pat the leaves dry. Chop the watercress fine.

Dice the water chestnuts.

In a bowl, combine the soy sauce, sesame seed oil, salt, and sugar, and mix thoroughly. Add the watercress and water chestnuts and toss until they are well coated with the sauce. Chill and serve.

Oil and Vinegar Dressing

3 tablespoons oil
1 tablespoon vinegar
Salt, pepper, and paprika to taste

Pour oil into a bottle with a tightly fitting lid. Add the vinegar, salt, pepper, and paprika. Shake vigorously to blend. Pour over salad.

For convenience, this dressing may be made in larger amounts and stored in the refrigerator for up to a week. Remove ½ hour before serving and let stand at room temperature. Shake well to blend ingredients.

Variations: Use olive oil, peanut oil, sesame seed oil, or any vegetable oil.

Use cider vinegar, apple cider, white vinegar, or wine vinegar. Or use a flavored vinegar: garlic, malt, tarragon, spiced, and so on. Lemon juice may be used in place of vinegar.

Olive Oil and Honey Dressing

2 tablespoons olive oil
2 tablespoons honey
1 tablespoon lemon juice
Seasonings as desired

Place all ingredients into a jar with a tight-fitting lid, and close it securely. Shake hard to combine the oil, honey, and lemon juice. This tasty dressing can be made either in larger quantities and stored or in individual servings. Adjust the tartness or sweetness to your taste by increasing the amount of lemon juice or honey you add.

Variations: Add a small clove of pressed garlic, finely sliced green onion, finely sliced radish, or a variety of herbs.

Marinate sliced vegetables in this dressing ½ hour to an hour or even longer. Then, pour it over salad greens.

Roquefort or Blue Cheese Dressing

¼ cup mayonnaise, sour cream, or cream cheese
2 to 4 tablespoons crumbled Roquefort or blue cheese
Dash of Worcestershire sauce (optional)
Dash of garlic powder and onion powder (optional)
2 teaspoons (approximately) milk

If using cream cheese, have it at room temperature. In a small bowl, combine the mayonnaise (or sour cream or cream cheese) and the Roquefort or blue cheese. Stir to soften and blend. Add the Worcestershire sauce, garlic powder, and onion powder. Add milk, a few drops at a time, and stir until desired consistency is reached. This dressing should be quite thick but still pour easily. Serve over green salad or fruit salad.

Ruby Salad Dressing

2 tablespoons olive oil
2 tablespoons tomato sauce
2 tablespoons cider vinegar
Dash of garlic powder *or* ¼ clove fresh garlic, mashed
⅛ teaspoon onion salt
⅛ teaspoon garlic salt
1 teaspoon sugar

Combine all ingredients in a jar with a tight-fitting top and shake well. Use on salads, or with sliced beets, or cooked and drained green beans.

Russian Dressing

2 tablespoons mayonnaise, sour cream, or yogurt
2 tablespoons catsup or bottled chili sauce
Dash onion powder

Combine all ingredients and mix well. Serve on green salad, mixed tossed salad, or chilled cooked vegetables.

Yogurt or Sour Cream Dressing

¼ cup yogurt or sour cream
2 tablespoons fruit juice (such as pineapple or orange juice)
Salt to taste

Place the yogurt or sour cream in a small bowl. Gradually add the fruit juice and stir. The quantity of juice needed depends on how thin you want the dressing.

Variation: For fruit salad, add a dash of nutmeg or cinnamon. For green salad, add a dash of garlic powder or onion powder.

10

Poultry

Aunt Mildred's Oven-Fried Chicken

2 or 3 pieces of chicken (breasts, thighs, legs, or wings) or desired
  quantity
Oil for dipping chicken
Flour, seasoned with salt and pepper

Preheat oven to 350° F.

Wash and pat dry the chicken pieces. Dip the pieces in oil, or
brush oil over each piece. Dip the pieces in the seasoned flour. Place
them on an oiled pan, such as a cookie sheet (not an open-end sheet).
Bake for about 25 to 30 minutes, depending on the thickness of the
chicken pieces you use.

To test for doneness, make a small slit in a thick part of the meat.
If the juice runs out clear, the chicken is cooked. It should be nicely
browned. Serve immediately.

Crusty Fried Chicken

2 or 3 pieces of chicken (breasts, thighs, legs, or wings) or desired
  quantity
Seasoned flour
¼ to ½ cup buttermilk
½ to ¾ cup fine bread crumbs
Oil (enough to cover chicken at least halfway)
Seasoned salt to taste

Shake chicken pieces in a bag of seasoned flour; then shake each piece
to remove excess and lay pieces on a piece of wax paper to dry, about 5
minutes.

Pour buttermilk into a shallow bowl or soup plate. Into another
similar dish pour the bread crumbs.

When the flour has adhered to the chicken pieces, dip each piece
into the buttermilk, then into the bread crumbs. Set aside to dry for
about 15 or 20 minutes. Again, dip the chicken pieces into the buttermilk and then into the bread crumbs. Let stand for a few more minutes.

Heat oil in a heavy skillet until hot but not smoking. Carefully
add the chicken pieces and fry. When a crust has formed on one side,
turn and cook the other side until a crust forms. Lower the heat to
moderate and cook until chicken is done, about 20 minutes. To test for
doneness, make a slit near the bone, or into the center of the meat; if
meat is pink, let chicken cook longer. The chicken should be medium
brown in color and will be quite juicy inside, yet crunchy on the outside. Sprinkle the pieces with seasoned salt as soon as you remove
them from the oil. Place on paper toweling to drain before serving.

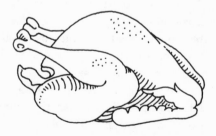

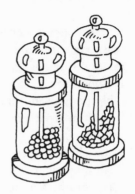

Deep-Fried Spring Chicken

Batter

4 tablespoons flour
4 tablespoons warm water
2 teaspoons vegetable oil
2 egg whites

(*Note:* If you wish to fry half a chicken, double this batter recipe.)

3 pieces of chicken: thigh, wing and drumstick
2 cups oil (approximately) for cooking
Seasoned salt

Mix flour, water, and oil to a smooth paste. Beat egg whites until stiff, then fold into batter. Batter should be thick. If it appears too thick, add a bit more water.

Wash and dry the chicken. Pour enough oil into a skillet, wok, or straight-side deep pan to cover the chicken pieces. Heat the oil until it hazes over. Dip the chicken pieces into the batter, coating them heavily, then slip each piece carefully into the hot oil. Be sure the pieces are not touching. Fry until chicken is cooked and golden brown, about 15 to 25 minutes. Drain on paper towels. Sprinkle chicken pieces with seasoned salt as soon as you remove them from the oil.

Stir-Fried Chicken Breast with Hoisin Sauce

$\frac{1}{2}$ chicken breast, uncooked (cooked chicken breast can be substituted)
1 teaspoon cornstarch
1 teaspoon Chinese rice wine or pale dry sherry
1 teaspoon soy sauce
1 tablespoon peanut oil or other flavorless vegetable oil, divided
$\frac{1}{4}$ medium-sized green pepper, cored, seeded, and cut into $\frac{1}{2}$-inch squares
2 water chestnuts, chopped
4 fresh mushrooms, chopped
2 teaspoons hoisin sauce
1 tablespoon slivered almonds, cashews, or pecans (optional)

Cut chicken breast into small, bite-sized pieces. Put the pieces in a bowl and sprinkle with the cornstarch; toss until pieces are lightly dusted. Add wine and soy sauce, then toss again until the pieces are coated.

Heat half the oil in a small skillet. Add green peppers, water chestnuts, and mushrooms. Stir-fry rapidly 2 to 3 minutes. Remove vegetables and set aside. Put the remaining oil in the pan and heat. Add chicken and wine-soy sauce mixture. Stir-fry over high heat until chicken turns firm and white. Add hoisin sauce, stir well, and return the vegetables to the pan. Cook for 1 minute, stirring just enough to heat vegetables well. Remove from heat. Sprinkle with nuts, if desired. Serve with fried or boiled rice.

Chinese Fried Chicken

2 tablespoons soy sauce
1 tablespoon rice wine or pale dry sherry
1 teaspoon salt
$\frac{1}{2}$ teaspoon sugar
$\frac{1}{2}$ inch crushed, peeled fresh ginger *or* $\frac{1}{4}$ teaspoon powdered ginger
1 green onion, including top, cut into $1\frac{1}{2}$-inch pieces, *or* $\frac{1}{2}$ teaspoon onion powder
3 chicken thighs or breasts

Oil to cover chicken (1 to 3 cups depending on pan size and number of
   chicken parts)
½ cup flour

Combine soy sauce, wine, salt, sugar, ginger, and green onion in a bowl
large enough to hold the chicken parts. Stir until salt and sugar are dissolved. Add the chicken, turning until the pieces are well coated, then
let stand at room temperature at least 45 minutes, preferably longer.
   Pour the oil into a skillet, wok, or deep-fryer, enough to cover the
chicken parts. Heat until a haze forms over the oil or the deep-fry thermometer registers 375° F. Remove chicken from marinade and dry; discard marinade. Dredge chicken in flour. Shake off excess flour and
carefully slip the chicken into the oil. Cook, turning frequently, for
about 5 minutes, until golden brown on all sides. Remove chicken and
drain on a double thickness of paper towels.

Braised Soy Sauce Chicken

½ cup cold water
½ cup soy sauce
1 tablespoon Chinese rice wine or pale dry sherry
2 slices fresh ginger root *or* preserved ginger, ¹⁄₁₆ inch to ⅛ inch thick
¼ teaspoon powdered anise *or* anise seed
½ chicken breast (or 2 thighs, legs, or wings)
1½ teaspoons sugar
Sesame seed oil or other oil for brushing chicken pieces

Use a covered saucepan just large enough to hold chicken pieces snug-
ly. Put water, soy sauce, wine, ginger, and anise into the pan, stir and
bring to a boil, then add chicken pieces. Liquid should reach halfway
up the chicken pieces. Bring to another boil, then reduce to moderate
heat. Cover and cook for 20 minutes. Turn pieces over, add sugar, and
baste pieces well. Simmer for 20 minutes more, basting often. Turn off
heat, cover the pot, and let stand for 30 to 45 minutes. Remove chicken
to serving dish and brush with oil. Sauce may be kept in a covered jar
in the refrigerator for about 2 weeks and indefinitely in the freezer.

Parmesan Chicken

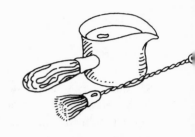

4 tablespoons fine bread crumbs
4 tablespoons grated Parmesan cheese
$\frac{1}{8}$ teaspoon seasoned salt (optional)
$\frac{3}{4}$ teaspoon paprika
$\frac{1}{2}$ tablespoon minced fresh parsley
$\frac{1}{8}$ teaspoon garlic powder
3 large chicken thighs
1 tablespoon butter or margarine, melted
$\frac{1}{4}$ teaspoon lemon juice

Preheat oven to 350° F.

Mix bread crumbs, Parmesan cheese, salt, paprika, parsley, and garlic powder. Dip chicken pieces into melted butter and roll in bread crumb mixture. Place in casserole that has a cover. Sprinkle the lemon juice on the chicken. Cover and bake for 1 hour without turning chicken pieces. To see whether chicken is done, make a small slit next to the bone. If meat is white, chicken is thoroughly cooked.

Herbed Chicken

1 large chicken breast or other chicken pieces in desired quantity
Italian herb seasoning *or* a mixture of marjoram, thyme, oregano, basil, rosemary, sage, and savory
Celery seed
Lemon Pepper
$\frac{1}{2}$ bunch fresh parsley, chopped, including stems

Preheat oven to 400° F.

Line a shallow 9-inch by 9-inch glass baking dish with foil. Put chicken pieces in baking dish and sprinkle generously on all sides with the herbs, celery seed, and Lemon Pepper. Cover all with the chopped parsley.

Bake for about 50 minutes, turning once or twice during the interim, until chicken is well cooked and lightly browned.

The abundant fresh parsley is the secret of the tantalizing flavor of this chicken dish.

Chicken Kiev (Stuffed Chicken Breast)

$\frac{1}{4}$ cup grated Parmesan cheese
$\frac{3}{4}$ cup fine bread crumbs
1 or 2 chicken breast halves
Unsalted butter or margarine, about $\frac{1}{2}$ tablespoon for each piece of chicken
Lemon Pepper to taste
Crushed tarragon to taste
Flour to taste
1 egg, beaten
Oil for deep frying

To make Parmesan bread crumbs: Add Parmesan cheese to bread crumbs and mix to blend well. (This keeps well in a tightly covered jar on the pantry shelf, so if you make more than you need you can use it later for breading.)

Skin each chicken breast, remove the fatty parts, then debone it. Pound the pieces flat on both sides.

Lay a piece of chilled butter in the center of each chicken fillet. Sprinkle heavily with Lemon Pepper and tarragon leaves. Fold the two short ends of the chicken over the butter, then the third and fourth sides, to form an envelope. If the chicken does not stay together, fasten with toothpicks.

Roll the pieces in flour, then dip in egg, and, finally, roll them in the bread crumbs. Set the pieces in the refrigerator while you heat the oil. Using a skillet, a deep-fat fryer, or a wok, heat the oil to about 350° F. When it is hot, using tongs, place the stuffed chicken in the oil and cook about 5 or 6 minutes, until golden brown on all sides. (You may have to turn the pieces once during the cooking process if you use the wok or skillet, and the oil is about an inch deep in the center of the wok.) If you don't use a deep fryer, the oil should be the depth of at least half the height of the chicken roll. Drain on paper towels.

Serve with rice or very thin French fries and a vegetable.

Chicken Marengo

This makes an excellent dish to take to work for lunch. Why not double the recipe and prepare tomorrow's lunch tonight?

2 or 3 chicken thighs
Seasoned flour
Oil for browning
½ clove garlic, minced, or ½ teaspoon garlic powder
1 teaspoon Bouquet Garni (see Note below)
¼ cup dry white wine
½ large (or 1 small) tomato cut into small pieces
2 fresh mushrooms, sliced
1 or 2 sprigs fresh parsley, chopped

Preheat oven to 350° F.

Dredge the chicken in the flour and shake off the excess. Heat the oil in a skillet, then add the chicken and brown until golden in color, turning frequently, using a high heat. Transfer the chicken to a casserole; add the garlic, Bouquet Garni, wine, and tomatoes. Cover tightly (use heavy foil crimped around the edges if you do not have a cover). Bake for about 30 minutes, then add the mushrooms and continue cooking until chicken is tender, another 10 or 15 minutes. Remove Bouquet Garni and serve sprinkled with parsley.

Note: You can buy Bouquet Garni in individual prepared bags. If you have the ready-mixed kind loose, put 1 teaspoon of prepared Garni in a metal tea ball and add this to the casserole. If you prefer to make your own bouquet, use 1 sprig each of fresh parsley and fresh thyme, a small stalk of celery and a bay leaf, all tied together with string. Other herbs may also be added, such as fennel, marjoram, tarragon, leeks, or green onion. I find the pulverized Garni and the metal tea ball is the easiest and quickest to use.

The casserole may be cooked on top of the stove, as long as you use a flameproof casserole dish.

Chicken Teriyaki

2 chicken thighs, wings, or breasts
6 tablespoons soy sauce
2 tablespoons sugar
2 tablespoons dry sherry or white rice wine
1 teaspoon grated fresh ginger root *or* $\frac{1}{2}$ teaspoon powdered ginger
$\frac{1}{2}$ small clove garlic, crushed, *or* $\frac{1}{4}$ teaspoon garlic powder

Preheat oven to 400° F.

Wash and pat the chicken dry. Pierce all over, using a table fork.

In a medium-sized bowl, mix all other items together and stir until the sugar is completely dissolved. Marinate the chicken in the sauce for at least 1 hour—overnight if possible. Turn the pieces from time to time.

Place the chicken in a shallow baking pan, reserving the marinade, and cook in the oven about 30 minutes. Meat is done when it is nicely browned and the juice runs clear when the meat is pierced.

Teriyaki Rice

Use the reserved marinade as part of the liquid for preparing rice in the standard fashion. Reduce the cooking water by the equivalent amount of marinade. The sauce will give the rice an interesting flavor and tint it a light brown color.

Baked Turkey Wing Puerto Rican Style

1 turkey wing or drumstick
½ clove garlic *or* ¼ teaspoon garlic powder
2 tablespoons minced onion *or* ¼ teaspoon onion powder
Black pepper and salt to taste
Oil to make a paste
Butter, margarine, or oil for basting
Wine

Preheat oven to 350° F.

Using a meat fork or sharp knife, poke holes all over the turkey. Mash the garlic, onion, pepper, and salt to a paste. Add sufficient oil to the paste to make ¼ to ½ cup—enough to thoroughly cover the turkey part. Rub the mixture into the turkey. Place the turkey on a piece of foil large enough to amply cover it, and pinch foil edges together. Bake about 1 hour, till tender.

During the baking, baste turkey every 15 to 20 minutes: open foil and rub the turkey with butter or oil, then baste with the wine, using a bulb-type baster or spoon to baste drippings over and into meat. About 10 minutes before turkey is done, open foil to brown meat.

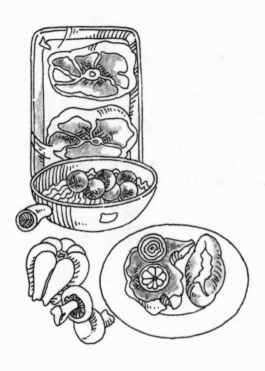

11

Meat

French-Fried Round Steak

1 piece round steak (4 or 5 ounces), pounded on both sides
Seasoned flour
Oil for frying

Pound the meat thoroughly. Then dip into seasoned flour and set aside for 10 to 15 minutes. Place enough oil in a wok or skillet to cover the meat while it is cooking. Heat the oil. If the meat has a rim of fat, score it diagonally to prevent curling. When oil is hot, carefully slide the meat into it and cook for about 2 minutes. Test for doneness by removing the meat to a plate and cutting it to see if it is cooked to the degree you wish. If not, return the meat to the hot oil for several more seconds.

Steak Smothered in Onions or Mushrooms

For this recipe you can use many different kinds of steak—round steak, sirloin, T-bone, porterhouse, rib—either beef or veal. The steak may be cooked by several different methods, which we give below.

While the steak is cooking, prepare the recipe for Creamed or Fried Onions (p. 143) or Creamed or Sautéed Mushrooms (pp. 139, 140). Pour over cooked steak and serve immediately.

To pan-broil

Use a heavy skillet, preferably the good old cast-iron type, large enough to hold the steak you are going to cook. Heat the pan until hot. There are two methods to determine this:

1. Heat the pan a short time, then drop a few drops of cold water into it. It is hot enough to use when the water dances on the pan and disappears almost immediately.

2. Sprinkle salt into the cold pan. When the salt begins to turn brown, the pan is ready to use. (If it turns dark brown, it is too hot.)

When the pan is hot, put the meat in and sear it for a second or two on one side, then turn and sear it on the other side. Lower the heat a bit and continue cooking until done. Drain off any fat that accumulates.

To determine whether it is done, check the amount of juice that rises to the top of the piece of meat. A few drops on the surface indicate the meat is rare; more drops indicate the meat is cooked more thoroughly. A lot of juice that also begins to disappear indicates the meat is well cooked. You can also cut into the meat in the thickest part and check the color of the inside. Red indicates rare, pink is medium, and brownish-gray is well done.

To fry

Frying a steak is much the same as pan-broiling except that you add fat to the pan before you cook the steak. Heat the oil before adding the meat, and cook over moderate heat. Fat can be butter, margarine, cooking oil, or a piece of fat trimmed from the meat and cooked until the oil escapes and covers the pan.

To broil

To cook steak in the broiler unit of the stove, remove the broiler pan to prevent the meat from sticking to it when hot, and preheat the broiler unit. Place meat on pan and broil according to the following chart:

	Distance from heat	Approximate cooking time for each side (for a ¾-inch steak)
Rare	2 inches	6 to 7 minutes
Medium	2 inches	10 minutes
Well Done	5 inches	12 to 15 minutes

When the first side is browned, turn the meat, using tongs, so as not to puncture the meat, and brown the other side. Season with salt and pepper as desired—after it is cooked.

To cook steak on a charcoal grill or a hibachi, let the charcoal get very hot. Place the meat on the grill and cook until tiny drops of juice appear on the surface. The more drops of juice, the better done the steak. For rare steak, only a few drops should appear. Turn meat and cook the other side until the juice rises to the top again. For rare steak, remove when only a few drops of juice appear; for well-done steak, cook until juice drops are evaporated.

Tournedos with Tomato Wine Sauce

¼ cup sliced mushrooms
1½ teaspoons butter or margarine
1 teaspoon minced shallots or green onions
¼ cup dry white wine
6 tablespoons stock
¼ cup tomato sauce (or 2 tablespoons tomato paste and 2 tablespoons water)
⅛ to ¼ teaspoon cornstarch, dissolved in small amount of water or stock
¼ tablespoon minced parsley
1 piece filet mignon, beef tenderloin or eye of round,* cut 1½ inches thick and about 2 inches across

In a skillet, sauté the mushrooms in butter, about 5 minutes. Add shallots, wine, stock, and tomato sauce. Simmer 5 minutes to blend the flavors. Stir the dissolved cornstarch into the sauce. Cook, stirring constantly, until sauce thickens and is smooth. Add the parsley.

Grill, broil, or fry the filet a few minutes on each side, enough to brown nicely, yet be medium rare, or to desired degree of doneness. (See directions for cooking steak, pp. 76, 77.) Season after cooking, if desired. Remove meat to a plate and pour the sauce over the meat.

*If using eye of round, marinate in dry red wine about an hour to tenderize.

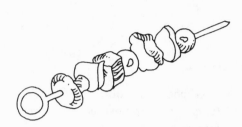

Skewered Beef with Vegetables

2 tablespoons canned pineapple juice
1 tablespoon distilled white vinegar or cider vinegar
1½ teaspoons dark molasses
Freshly ground black pepper to taste
Salt to taste
½ pound cubed beef, such as top sirloin
3 boiling onions, unpeeled
1 medium tomato, quartered
¼ green pepper, cored, seeded, and cut into cubes
1 or 2 small zucchini, cut into chunks about ½ to ¾ inch thick

In a large bowl, mix the pineapple juice, vinegar, and molasses; add the black pepper, salt, and meat cubes. Marinate at room temperature for 1 hour, turning the meat occasionally.

Parboil the onions in a saucepan for about 10 minutes and slip off the skins.

Preheat an electric grill, broiler, or charcoal grill. When hot, remove the meat pieces from the marinade (reserve marinade for basting) and thread them on a skewer, pushing them closely together. Thread the vegetables on another skewer, alternating the vegetables or grouping them all together.

Set the skewers about 4 inches from the heat. Turn frequently and baste them with the marinade. Watch the vegetables carefully so they won't burn; they may cook faster than the meat.

When all is cooked, slide the pieces onto your plate. This dish is good served with rice.

Variation: Quarter a 2-inch mushroom and add to the vegetables. Or try almost any vegetable that cooks rather quickly.

Shish Kebab

Marinade

1 tablespoon olive oil
1 teaspoon onion powder
1 teaspoon chili powder
Dash powdered ginger
1/8 to 1/4 teaspoon garlic powder
2 tablespoons vinegar
Dash cinnamon
Dash freshly ground pepper
3/4 teaspoon brown sugar
2 tablespoons red wine

4 to 5 chunks of lean beef, lamb, or pork, about 2 inches square

Any 2 or 3 of the following:
2 large fresh mushrooms, quartered
1 small green pepper, cored and seeded and cut in 2-inch squares
1 small tomato, quartered
3 to 4 small white (boiling size) onions or 1 small yellow onion, quartered

Combine all marinade ingredients. Put the meat cubes in the marinade and let stand 1 to 2 hours. Preheat grill or broiler about 15 minutes prior to cooking time. Arrange the meat cubes and vegetables alternately on a long skewer, brush with the marinade, and then broil, turning frequently, until the meat and vegetables are cooked. Serve on a bed of fluffy rice, seasoned with a bouillon cube if you desire.

If you would like to use all of the vegetables mentioned, place the meat on one skewer and the vegetables on another, or alternate meat and vegetables on two or more skewers, being careful to not crowd them. During cooking, leave room enough for the heat to circulate on all sides of each skewer. The vegetables will cook in less time than the meat.

Beef Stroganoff

½ pound sirloin or round steak, all fat removed, cut in 1-inch cubes
Flour for dredging
½ cup chopped onions
2 to 3 fresh mushrooms, sliced thin, *or* a small can of small button
  mushrooms or stems and pieces
2 tablespoons olive oil or butter or margarine
Salt and pepper to taste
Paprika to taste
1 bouillon cube
½ teaspoon tomato paste
½ to ¾ cup commercial sour cream

Dredge meat cubes in flour and set aside for ½ hour. In a skillet, sauté onions and mushrooms in oil or butter (or both). Remove onions and mushrooms from pan, add a bit more oil if necessary, and cook the meat until brown on all sides, stirring frequently. Add salt, pepper, paprika, bouillon cube, and tomato paste and blend. Check seasoning for taste; it should be very spicy, because no further seasoning should be added after the sour cream. Add the onions and mushrooms, then stir in the sour cream. Continue to stir over low heat until sour cream melts down and coats the meat, but do not boil. Simmer over low heat for 30 to 45 minutes to blend the flavors. If you like extra sauce (and it's delicious for dipping pieces of warm French bread into), add a bit more sour cream at the beginning. You may use as much as a full cup of sour cream.

Serve with rice or buttered noodles.

Stir-Fried Steak with Mushrooms and Bean Sprouts

1 tablespoon oil
$\frac{1}{4}$ pound steak, cut in 1-inch cubes
2 medium fresh mushrooms, sliced, *or* a few canned mushroom caps or
   stems and pieces
3 stalks fresh asparagus, cut in small pieces
1 to $1\frac{1}{2}$ cups bean sprouts, rinsed, drained, and patted dry
1 teaspoon fermented black beans (optional)
$\frac{1}{3}$ cup chicken broth
1 tablespoon soy sauce
1 teaspoon sugar
1 teaspoon cornstarch dissolved in a bit of water

Heat the oil in a skillet or wok. Add the meat and sauté till browned on
all sides. Add mushrooms and asparagus and cook about 2 minutes.
Add bean sprouts, fermented black beans (if desired), chicken broth,
soy sauce, and sugar. Simmer another 1 to 2 minutes, then add the dissolved cornstarch. Stir gently until the meat and vegetables are coated
and the cornstarch has thickened the sauce, about 1 minute. Serve with
fluffy rice.

Stir-Fried Steak and Vegetables

2 dried Chinese mushrooms, 1 inch to $1\frac{1}{2}$ inches in diameter, quartered
   and soaked for 30 minutes in $\frac{1}{2}$ cup warm water, *or* 2 fresh mushrooms, quartered
2 ounces snow peas, fresh or frozen and thoroughly defrosted
$\frac{1}{2}$ pound lean, tender beef (top sirloin, tenderloin, or other)
$\frac{1}{2}$ teaspoon sugar
1 tablespoon soy sauce
$1\frac{1}{2}$ teaspoons rice wine or pale dry sherry
1 teaspoon cornstarch
$1\frac{1}{2}$ teaspoons oil, divided
3 water chestnuts, rinsed, drained, and sliced $\frac{1}{4}$ inch thick
$\frac{1}{4}$ teaspoon salt
2 slices peeled ginger root, 1 inch by $\frac{1}{8}$ inch, fresh or preserved

Soak mushrooms if you are using the dried variety. If using fresh pea pods, snap off the ends and remove strings from the pods, then drop them into a pan of boiling water. They will turn bright green in a minute. Drain and run cold water over them. If you are using frozen peas, they require no treatment.

Trim any fat from the meat, and cut meat into 1-inch cubes.

In a small bowl, combine the sugar, soy sauce, wine, and cornstarch. Mix thoroughly, then add the beef cubes, tossing them until they are well coated.

In a preheated skillet, pour in $\frac{1}{2}$ teaspoon of the oil, lowering the heat if the oil begins to smoke. Add the mushrooms, snow peas, and water chestnuts. Cook, stirring, over moderate heat for about 2 minutes, until they are coated with the oil. Add the salt, then remove the vegetables with a slotted spoon or skimmer and set aside.

Pour in the remaining teaspoon of oil and add the ginger. Turn the heat to high, and drop in the beef cubes. Stir-fry for 2 to 3 minutes, or until the cubes are lightly browned on all sides. Discard the ginger, and return the vegetables to the pan, stirring constantly for about 10 seconds, until they are heated through. Remove and serve with rice or buttered noodles.

Gingered Steak Strips

$\frac{1}{4}$ pound boneless round steak, $\frac{1}{2}$ inch thick
1 teaspoon butter or margarine
$\frac{1}{4}$ tablespoon coarsely chopped blanched almonds (optional)
$\frac{1}{2}$ teaspoon ginger powder
$\frac{1}{4}$ teaspoon chili powder
Dash of garlic powder
$\frac{3}{4}$ teaspoon minced or powdered onion
$\frac{1}{3}$ teaspoon beef stock base
$\frac{1}{2}$ cup hot water
$\frac{1}{2}$ teaspoon plum jam
$\frac{1}{2}$ teaspoon red wine vinegar
$\frac{1}{2}$ teaspoon cornstarch, dissolved in $\frac{1}{2}$ teaspoon cold water
1 teaspoon sherry

Cut steak into $\frac{1}{2}$-inch strips. In a heavy skillet, brown the meat lightly in butter. Add almonds, if desired, ginger, chili powder, garlic powder, and minced or powdered onion and stir into meat. Dissolve beef stock base in hot water and pour into pan. Add plum jam and vinegar. Cover and simmer until meat is tender, 15 to 20 minutes. Add cornstarch mixture and stir. When sauce is thick and transparent, add sherry. Serve hot with rice.

Spiced Beef and Snow Peas

$\frac{1}{4}$ cup soy sauce
$\frac{1}{4}$ cup tempura sauce
$\frac{1}{4}$ cup chicken stock
$\frac{1}{4}$ cup sherry or white wine
3 teaspoons sugar
Dash of garlic powder
Dash of powdered ginger
1 tablespoon oil
4 ounces of beef, sliced $\frac{1}{8}$ inch thick, then crosswise into pieces about
    $1\frac{1}{2}$ inches long

½ package frozen snow peas *or* a handful of fresh snow peas, deribbed and washed but not shelled
1 teaspoon cornstarch dissolved in a small amount of cold water or stock

Combine soy and tempura sauces, stock, wine, sugar, garlic powder, and ginger. Add the meat and marinate ½ hour or longer.

Drain the meat, reserving the marinade. Heat oil in a skillet or wok, add meat, and stir-fry just until brown. Add 1 cup of the marinade and bring to a boil. Add peas. Cook, stirring, for 1 to 2 minutes. Add dissolved cornstarch and stir until the sauce thickens and becomes transparent.

Serve with fluffy boiled rice.

Stir-Fried Flank Steak with Fresh Asparagus

4 ounces flank steak (or substitute other steak)
1 teaspoon cornstarch
2 tablespoons soy sauce, chicken broth, or water
1 tablespoon peanut oil or other flavorless vegetable oil
5 to 6 stalks fresh asparagus, cut on the diagonal into 2-inch pieces
2 green onions, cut on the diagonal into 2-inch pieces
½ cup bean sprouts, washed and drained
1 teaspoon fermented black beans

Cut the steak, with the grain, into strips ½ inch wide, then cut these strips into pieces 1 inch to 1½ inches long. Mix the cornstarch with the liquid. Heat the oil in a skillet or wok for a minute or so, swirling it around in the pan. If the oil begins to smoke, lower the heat to moderate. Drop in the meat and stir-fry until it loses its pink color. Add the asparagus, green onion, and bean sprouts, and stir-fry for 2 to 3 minutes. Add the black beans, and stir once or twice to blend them into the mixture. Stir cornstarch mixture quickly to recombine it, then add it to the pan. Stir until the sauce thickens and becomes transparent. Remove to a plate and serve.

Chinese Pepper Steak

½ pound tender steak (flank, top sirloin, porterhouse, T-bone, or rib)
1½ teaspoons rice wine or pale dry sherry
4½ teaspoons soy sauce
½ teaspoon sugar
1 teaspoon cornstarch
2 tablespoons peanut oil, divided
1 medium-sized green pepper, cored, seeded, and cut into ½-inch squares
2 slices peeled ginger root, 1 inch by ⅛ inch, fresh or preserved

Cut the meat lengthwise into strips 1½ inches wide, then cut these strips into ¼-inch-thick slices.

Mix the wine, soy sauce, sugar, and cornstarch in a bowl, and add the meat pieces. Toss with a spoon to coat them thoroughly. You can marinate the meat in the sauce or cook it immediately.

Heat 2 teaspoons oil in a skillet for several seconds. If the oil begins to smoke, lower the heat to moderate. Add the green pepper and stir-fry for about 3 minutes, until it is tender but still crisp. Remove pepper with a slotted spoon or skimmer and set aside. Pour in the rest of the oil and heat almost to the smoking point, then add the ginger and stir for a few seconds. Drop in the meat mixture. Stir-fry over high heat for a couple of minutes or until the meat no longer appears pink. Discard the ginger. Return the peppers to the pan and cook for 1 to 2 minutes, stirring. Remove to a plate and serve.

Beef Stew with Mushrooms

¼ pound stewing beef
½ can undiluted cream of mushroom soup
2 teaspoons dry onion soup mix
2 tablespoons sherry
1 large or 2 medium-sized fresh mushrooms, diced
4 to 6 small fresh boiling onions
1 medium-sized carrot, cubed
¼ cup frozen peas

In a Dutch oven, combine the raw beef, mushroom soup, onion soup mix, and sherry. Bake for 2 to 2¼ hours at 325° F. Add mushrooms, onions, and carrots, and continue to bake until meat is tender, about 30 minutes. Add the peas and cook 5 to 10 minutes longer. Makes one hearty serving.

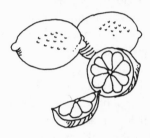

Meatballs with Lemon Sauce

¼ pound ground beef
½ tablespoon chopped onion *or* ¼ teaspoon onion powder
1 tablespoon uncooked rice
1 tablespoon plus 1 teaspoon tomato paste
¼ teaspoon chopped parsley
Salt and pepper to taste
1 cup beef stock (1 bouillon cube dissolved in 1 cup water)
1 egg
½ tablespoon water
1 tablespoon lemon juice

Mix the ground beef, onion, rice, tomato paste, parsley, salt, and pepper until well blended. Shape into balls.

Heat the stock in a saucepan or skillet and when it boils, gently drop in the meatballs, a few at a time. Cover the pan and simmer about 20 to 30 minutes, depending on the size of the meatballs.

To prepare the sauce, beat the egg and water until fluffy in the top of a double boiler. Gradually add 1½ teaspoons hot stock and the lemon juice and stir over low heat. As soon as sauce begins to thicken, remove from the heat. Let stand about 5 minutes before serving.

Transfer meatballs to a plate and pour the lemon sauce over them. Serve with rice and zucchini.

Sour Cream Meatballs

1 slice of bread, crumbled fine
2 tablespoons milk
¼ pound ground beef
2 green onions, sliced thin
¼ teaspoon salt
⅛ teaspoon pepper
Oil or shortening for browning
¼ cup sour cream
Paprika to taste

Preheat oven to 350° F.

In a bowl, mix the bread crumbs with the milk. When crumbs are moistened, add the meat, onions, salt, and pepper, and form into small balls about the size of a large walnut. Heat the oil in a skillet. When oil is hot, add the meatballs and brown, rolling the balls around frequently to avoid flat sides. When browned on all sides, transfer the meatballs to a small casserole. Spread the sour cream over the meatballs and sprinkle generously with paprika. Cover the casserole and bake for 25 minutes.

Serve with Noodles Romanoff (see p. 151).

Ground Meat Roll with Vegetable Filling

¼ to ½ pound ground meat, lean
2 mushrooms, 1½ to 2 inches in diameter, washed or wiped with a
    damp towel
3 to 4 water chestnuts
2 green onions, washed
1 handful bean sprouts, drained
Lemon Pepper, salt, and pepper to taste

Preheat oven to 400° F.

On a piece of wax paper, form the meat into a rectangle about ½ inch thick. Slice the mushrooms about ¼ inch thick, and place them across the top of the meat. Slice the water chestnuts in thin slices, the green onions in ½-inch pieces. Distribute them over the top of the meat and mushrooms. Scatter the drained bean sprouts over this. Sprinkle with the Lemon Pepper, salt, and pepper. Using the wax paper as a pusher, roll the meat, jelly-roll fashion, starting from the narrow end. Remove the paper and place the roll in a greased metal or glass baking dish, seam side down. Bake for about 30 minutes.

Other Filling Suggestions

"Country" style: Mix a little packaged poultry stuffing with meat broth (fresh, canned, granulated, or made from extract or a beef bouillon cube).

"South-of-the-border" style: Combine chopped onions, chopped green pepper, tomato slices, and a layer of leftover rice, either plain or seasoned. Season with chili powder, salt, and pepper.

"Hawaiian" style: Add some pineapple bits, either fresh or canned (and drained) along with sliced green pepper, sliced white or green onions, little sweet pickles thinly sliced, and 2 water chestnuts, sliced.

Or whatever else you happen to think of that will make an interesting combination of tastes, textures, and colors ... and use up some of those odds and ends in the refrigerator.

Meat Loaf

½ pound ground beef
1 egg
¾ teaspoon cornstarch
¼ teaspoon onion powder *or* ¼ medium onion, minced
⅛ cup milk, scalded
1 tablespoon fine bread crumbs
Pinch of nutmeg
Pinch of allspice
Pinch of ginger

Preheat oven to 400° F.

Mix all the ingredients together until evenly mixed and light in texture. Place mixture in a greased 3-inch by 6-inch by 2-inch individual loaf pan. Bake for approximately 30 minutes.

Serve plain or with a gravy made from the pan drippings. Or use mushroom sauce or chili sauce, if desired.

Superb Hamburger

$\frac{1}{4}$ pound ground sirloin or other lean beef
$\frac{1}{2}$ tomato, peeled, seeded, and chopped (reserve juice)
$1\frac{1}{2}$ teaspoons chopped onion *or* $\frac{1}{8}$ teaspoon onion powder
1 tablespoon chopped bell pepper *or* $\frac{1}{4}$ teaspoon dehydrated bell pepper
$\frac{3}{4}$ teaspoon capers
$\frac{1}{3}$ teaspoon oregano
1 tablespoon flour (for dusting meat)
1 tablespoon butter, margarine, shortening, or oil
8 teaspoons white wine
1 tablespoon chopped parsley

Mix the ground beef, tomato, onion, pepper, capers, and oregano, and shape into a roll or patty. Dust very lightly with flour. (Flour should be barely visible.) Heat the butter or oil in heavy skillet and, when hot, add patty and cook until browned well on both sides (about 10 to 14 minutes). If you shape the beef into a roll be sure to turn it frequently while cooking to avoid a "flat" side. Mix the wine with the tomato juice and pour over the meat. Simmer for about 5 minutes. Serve, pouring the sauce over the meat, and then sprinkle the top with chopped parsley.

Special Ground Sirloin Steak

$\frac{1}{3}$ to $\frac{1}{2}$ pound ground sirloin
Lemon Pepper
1 to 2 green onions, including tops, thinly sliced
1 medium-sized fresh mushroom, diced, *or* $\frac{1}{2}$ small can button mushrooms, drained

Mix the ground sirloin with the Lemon Pepper and shape into a patty. Press part of the chopped green onions and mushrooms into the meat patty on both sides. Pan-broil. When the meat is cooked, sprinkle the remaining green onions and mushrooms over the top of the patty and serve.

Braised Lamb with Sour Cream

1 lamb shoulder chop, boned
½ tablespoon flour
Dash garlic powder
Dash of black pepper
¼ teaspoon salt
1 teaspoon beef stock base (or part of a bouillon cube)
½ cup hot water
½ tablespoon minced onion (fresh or instant)
⅛ teaspoon Bouquet Garni
¼ tablespoon garlic wine vinegar
¼ cup dairy sour cream (or more if desired)

Trim fat from meat and cut into cubes. Lightly grease a heavy skillet, using a piece of the fat or a bit of olive oil. Combine the flour, garlic powder, pepper, and salt, and coat each piece of meat in the flour mixture. Shake off excess flour and reserve. Brown the meat slowly in the skillet, then remove. Skim off excess fat, leaving only a few drippings. Stir in remaining flour and brown lightly. Dissolve the beef stock or bouillon cube in hot water; add the onions. Pour mixture into the browned flour, stirring constantly. Cook until gravy is thickened.

Return the browned meat to the pan. Crush the Bouquet Garni and sprinkle over lamb. Stir in vinegar; cover and cook over low heat until meat is very tender—about 20 minutes.

Stir in sour cream and heat but do not boil. Serve immediately with buttered noodles, mashed potatoes, or steamed rice.

Lamb Shank in Barbecue Sauce

1 lamb shank
Salt and pepper to taste
2 tablespoons oil
¼ teaspoon garlic powder *or* 1 clove fresh garlic, minced
1 tablespoon onion powder *or* ¼ medium onion, minced
1 teaspoon Worcestershire sauce
1 teaspoon bottled barbecue sauce
1 tablespoon sherry or white wine
1 teaspoon red wine garlic vinegar
1 teaspoon sugar
Dash of celery seed or celery salt
1 tablespoon dehydrated green pepper *or* fresh green pepper, cored, seeded, and chopped fine

Trim the skin and fat from the lamb shank. Sprinkle with salt and pepper. In a skillet, brown the shank in oil over medium heat. When the shank is browned on all sides, remove from pan and reserve.

If you use fresh garlic or onion, add them to the skillet and cook them slightly in the remaining oil. Mix remaining ingredients in the same pan and simmer for 2 minutes. Return shank to the pan, cover, lower the heat, and simmer about 1½ hours. Turn the shank once or twice during the cooking period. Serve.

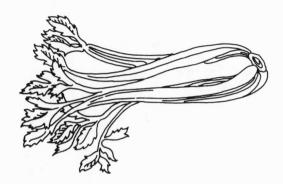

Lamb Shank Beaujolais

1 lamb shank, fat and membrane removed
1 tablespoon butter or margarine
1 tablespoon olive oil
$\frac{1}{8}$ cup chopped celery *or* $\frac{1}{4}$ teaspoon celery seed
$\frac{1}{2}$ medium onion, chopped, *or* $\frac{1}{2}$ teaspoon onion powder
Pinch of salt
Pinch of pepper
Pinch of rosemary
Pinch of sage
1 tablespoon tomato paste
$\frac{1}{2}$ cup Beaujolais wine (or any hearty red wine)
$\frac{1}{4}$ cup water or beef stock*
1 small clove garlic *or* $\frac{1}{4}$ to $\frac{1}{2}$ teaspoon garlic powder
Grated rind of $\frac{1}{2}$ small lemon *or* $\frac{1}{2}$ tablespoon bottled lemon peel
1 tablespoon chopped parsley or parsley flakes

In a skillet, brown the lamb shank in butter and oil. Add the celery, onion, salt, pepper, rosemary, and sage. Cover, and simmer 10 to 15 minutes.

Blend the tomato paste with the wine and stir into juices in the pot. Add the water or stock, cover, and simmer over low heat for about 1 hour. Add small amounts of liquid as necessary.

When meat is tender, sprinkle with the combined garlic, lemon peel, and parsley.

Serve with plain boiled rice or herbed rice.

*Beef stock can be made by dissolving 1 beef bouillon cube in 1 cup boiling water. Or crumble $\frac{1}{2}$ to 1 whole cube directly into the hot liquid in the pot.

Baked Lamb Shank Garni

1 lamb shank
½ teaspoon Bouquet Garni
½ teaspoon garlic powder
½ teaspoon ground ginger
Pepper to taste
½ teaspoon olive oil
¼ cup Cabernet Sauvignon or other red wine

Preheat oven to 375° F.

Using a cooking fork or small, sharp knife, punch holes all over the shank. Mix the Bouquet Garni, garlic powder, ginger, and pepper with the oil and rub into the meat, using all the mixture. Place in a covered baking dish and add the wine. Bake about 1 to 1½ hours, until brown and tender. Baste the meat several times during the cooking, turning it occasionally to brown evenly.

To serve, skim off the oil and spoon the thickened sauce over the shank. A baked potato goes well with this dish. It can bake in the oven along with the lamb shank.

Pineapple Lamb Shank

1 lamb shank
Olive oil for browning
¼ cup catsup
½ cup pineapple juice
2 dashes garlic powder *or* small clove of garlic, minced
2 dashes onion powder *or* about 2 tablespoons diced onion
¼ teaspoon Lemon Pepper

In a skillet, brown meat in olive oil until it is well browned on all sides. Pour off all but 1 tablespoon oil. Add the catsup, pineapple juice, and seasonings. Cover pan and cook meat over low heat for about 45 to 50 minutes, until done. Serve.

Easy Barbecued Spareribs

¼ cup prepared barbecue sauce
2 tablespoons molasses (or to taste)
3 to 5 large spareribs

Preheat oven to 350° F.

Pour barbecue sauce into a soup plate or other large shallow container (such as a pie pan), add the molasses, and stir. Taste for mellowness. You may wish to add more of the barbecue sauce or molasses, as suits your taste.

Place the ribs in the sauce and allow to marinate for a short while (30 minutes to 1 hour) if you have the time. Otherwise, brush the sauce over the ribs and bake until meat is well cooked and ribs are browned.

To avoid splattering the oven, place ribs on a rack set over the baking pan. Pour about a cup of water into the pan. The drippings will fall into the water and not splatter the oven or burn onto the pan.

Variations: Cook the ribs in any usual manner and at the last minute brush the sauce on, cooking just long enough to warm the sauce.

This sauce is also excellent on chicken. Pierce the skin of the chicken and allow pieces to marinate for a while for best results.

German Spareribs

3 or 4 spareribs
⅓ cup boiling water
½ teaspoon beef stock base
1 teaspoon tomato catsup
⅓ teaspoon brown sugar
1 teaspoon red wine vinegar
⅛ teaspoon ground allspice
Pinch of caraway seed
1 teaspoon Worcestershire Sauce
Few grains cayenne pepper
⅛ teaspoon lemon peel
¼ teaspoon cornstarch, dissolved in 1½ teaspoons water

Preheat oven to 350° F.

Cut ribs into serving pieces 1 inch to 2 inches long (ask the butcher to do this if possible). Place in a baking dish and bake for about 25 minutes, turning frequently. Drain off fat. Combine boiling water, beef stock base, catsup, brown sugar, vinegar, allspice, caraway seed, Worcestershire sauce, cayenne pepper, and lemon peel in a bowl. Pour over ribs and continue baking for about 20 minutes, turning frequently. When done, remove the ribs. Skim off fat from liquid in pan and add the cornstarch mixed in water. Stir constantly over low heat until liquid thickens. Pour over ribs. Serve.

Sweet and Pungent Spareribs

Ask the butcher to cut the ribs into bite-sized pieces, 1½ inches to 2 inches in length.

This is a dish you can cook, then divide into containers and freeze for future dinners. Or, if you prefer, you can prepare an individual serving. Measurements for both single and quantity servings are given below.

For 1

2 tablespoons peanut oil
3 or 4 spareribs, cut into 1-inch
  pieces
1 tablespoon chopped onion
1 tablespoon green pepper, cored,
  seeded, and chopped
1/4 cup pineapple juice
3 tablespoons cider vinegar
3 tablespoons water
1 teaspoon catsup
Few drops soy sauce
1 to 2 drops Worcestershire sauce
1/2 teaspoon minced garlic *or*
  generous dash garlic powder
1 1/2 tablespoons firmly packed
  brown sugar
1 teaspoon cornstarch

For 4 to 6

1/4 cup peanut oil
2 pounds spareribs, cut into 1-inch
  pieces
1/4 cup chopped onion
1/4 cup green pepper, cored,
  seeded, and chopped
1 cup pineapple juice
3/4 cup cider vinegar
3/4 cup water
2 tablespoons catsup
1 tablespoon soy sauce
1/4 teaspoon Worcestershire sauce
1 medium clove garlic, chopped
  fine
1/2 cup firmly packed brown sugar
2 tablespoons cornstarch

Heat the oil in a heavy skillet. Add the spareribs, and brown well. Remove the ribs and set aside. Pour off all but 2 teaspoons (2 tablespoons) of the drippings, then add the onion and green pepper and cook until tender. Add the pineapple juice, vinegar, water, catsup, soy sauce, Worcestershire sauce, and garlic. Blend the brown sugar and cornstarch in a cup with a bit of the liquid, then add it to the rest of the ingredients. Bring to a boil, stirring constantly. Reduce the heat, add the ribs, and cook, uncovered, over low heat until the ribs are tender. This will require about 1 hour, depending upon the thickness of the meat on the ribs. Stir occasionally. Serve with rice or baked beans.

This can also be cooked in a roaster in the oven at about 350° F.

Variation: Use pork riblets instead of spareribs. These riblets come in a strip about 8 inches long and 1/2 inch wide.

Spareribs with Peach Preserves

3 to 4 spareribs
1/4 cup peach preserves (or thick jam)
2 teaspoons brown sugar
1 teaspoon red wine garlic vinegar
2 to 3 drops Worcestershire sauce

Preheat oven to 500° F.

Place the ribs, still joined, in a shallow baking pan. Bake for about 10 minutes on each side until slightly browned. Remove from oven, drain off most of the grease. Lower heat to about 400° F.

Combine preserves, brown sugar, vinegar, and Worcestershire sauce. Spread over both sides of the ribs, and return ribs to the oven. Bake 20 to 30 minutes, depending on the thickness of the meat on the ribs.

Variation: Instead of peach preserves, substitute any type of citrus fruit preserves or jam, such as orange marmalade, apricot jam, pineapple-apricot, pineapple-peach, or plum jam.

Western Barbecued Spareribs

3 to 4 ribs (1 pound)
5 to 6 tablespoons tomato sauce
1 tablespoon water
1/4 tablespoon onion powder *or* 1 tablespoon minced onion
1/8 teaspoon garlic powder
1 1/3 teaspoons Worcestershire sauce
1/2 tablespoon red wine vinegar
1 1/3 teaspoons brown sugar
1/4 teaspoon honey
1/8 teaspoon dry mustard
1/8 teaspoon chili powder
1/4 teaspoon Liquid Smoke
1/4 teaspoon lemon juice

Preheat oven to 350° F.

Brown the ribs for about 30 to 45 minutes in a covered roasting pan, preferably placing the ribs on a rack inside the pan.

Mix the remaining ingredients in a saucepan, bring to a boil, lower the heat, and simmer for about 15 or 20 minutes. Stir frequently and do not let it become too thick.

At the end of the roasting time, uncover the pan, drain off the accumulated fat, and increase the heat to 425° F. Brush the ribs with the sauce and roast until fork tender, 30 to 45 minutes. Baste and turn the ribs frequently until they are done and nicely glazed.

If you separate the ribs at the end of the first roasting, using a sharp knife, the ribs will be covered with the sauce on all sides instead of just on the top and bottom.

Elegant Pork Chops

1 pork chop, with or without bone
1 thin slice onion
1 thin slice lemon *or* 1 teaspoon lemon juice
1 teaspoon brown sugar
1 teaspoon catsup
1 or 2 teaspoons water

Brown the chop on one side in a lightly greased skillet. Turn the chop when browned. Place the onion and lemon slice on the top (the unbrowned side). Sprinkle the brown sugar and catsup over the onion and exposed meat. Add the water and cover the pan tightly. Lower the flame and cook slowly for about 20 minutes, until the chop is tender and not pink inside.

A baked sweet potato is a good accompaniment; start it baking about 45 to 50 minutes before you prepare the chop.

Sweet and Sour Pork

$\frac{1}{2}$ pound lean, boneless pork, cut into 1-inch cubes
Oil for cooking, enough to fill pan 2 inches deep

Batter

1 egg, lightly beaten
1 teaspoon salt
$\frac{1}{4}$ cup cornstarch
$\frac{1}{4}$ cup flour
$\frac{1}{4}$ cup chicken stock, either fresh, canned, or made by dissolving
   bouillon cube in 1 cup boiling water

Sauce

$1\frac{1}{2}$ teaspoons peanut oil
2 teaspoons minced fresh garlic *or* $\frac{1}{4}$ teaspoon powdered garlic
$\frac{1}{2}$ large green pepper, cored, seeded, and cut into $\frac{1}{2}$-inch pieces
$\frac{1}{2}$ medium-sized carrot, scraped and sliced into 2-inch strips about $\frac{1}{4}$
   inch by $\frac{1}{4}$ inch wide and thick
$\frac{1}{4}$ cup chicken stock
2 tablespoons sugar
2 tablespoons red wine vinegar
$\frac{1}{2}$ teaspoon soy sauce
$1\frac{1}{2}$ teaspoons cornstarch dissolved in 1 tablespoon cold water

Place the cubed meat into a dish. Heat the oil in a skillet or wok. Combine the ingredients for the batter in a bowl. When the oil is hot (about 375° F. on a deep-fat thermometer), dip the meat cubes into the batter and stir to coat each piece well. Drop the coated cubes into the hot oil one by one, being careful not to splatter the oil or crowd the cubes. Cook 5 to 6 minutes, adjusting the heat so that the cubes will turn a crisp, golden brown without burning. Using a slotted spoon or skimmer, remove the cubes to a small baking dish and set in a warm oven to keep warm while you fry any remaining meat cubes and make the sauce.

To make the sauce: Pour the oil into a small saucepan and heat for about 30 seconds. Add the garlic, green pepper, and carrot, stirring 2 to 3 minutes until the pepper and carrot darken somewhat, being careful not to burn them. Pour in the chicken stock, sugar, vinegar, and soy sauce, and bring to a boil. Boil rapidly for 1 minute or until the sugar is thoroughly dissolved. Stir the cornstarch mixture briskly, then add it to the sauce, stirring constantly while it cooks. When it becomes thick and clear, either pour it over the cooked pork or place the pork in the sauce. Serve.

Note: Since the flavor of the sauce improves after it has stood for a day or more, you may wish to make the sauce ahead of time.

This recipe is good in larger quantities, too, for it is a tasty "make ahead" dish. It keeps well in a covered dish in the refrigerator for at least 3 days and is delicious reheated. To make in larger quantities, merely adjust the amount of pork you use and increase the sauce ingredients proportionately.

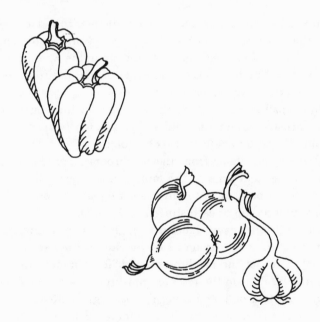

Stuffed Braised Mushrooms with Pork and Water Chestnuts

4 to 5 dried or fresh mushrooms, 1 inch to $1\frac{1}{2}$ inch in diameter
1 teaspoon soy sauce
1 teaspoon Chinese rice wine or pale dry sherry
$\frac{1}{8}$ teaspoon sugar
$\frac{1}{2}$ teaspoon cornstarch, divided
$\frac{1}{8}$ pound boneless pork shoulder, finely minced, *or* 1 pork chop, boned and minced
1 canned water chestnut, finely chopped, *or* 1 fresh water chestnut, peeled and chopped
4 to 5 small sprigs of parsley, Chinese (cilantro) or Italian
1 teaspoon peanut oil or other flavorless vegetable oil
2 teaspoons bottled oyster sauce

If you use the dried mushrooms, wipe them with a damp cloth, then place in a small bowl, cover with $\frac{1}{2}$ cup of warm water, and let soak for 30 minutes. Remove from water and strain the water through a fine sieve, saving 2 tablespoons of the water. If you use fresh mushrooms, wipe them clean with a damp paper towel.

In a small bowl, combine the soy sauce, wine, sugar, and $\frac{1}{4}$ teaspoon cornstarch, and stir until the cornstarch is dissolved. Add the pork and the water chestnut. Mix thoroughly.

Remove the stems from the mushrooms. Sprinkle a little cornstarch on the stem sides of the mushrooms. Then, fill the mushroom caps with the pork mixture, dividing it equally among them. Place a parsley sprig on top of each stuffed mushroom.

Heat oil in a heavy skillet over high heat for a few seconds. Arrange the stuffed mushrooms side by side in the pan. Lower heat to moderate, and let the mushrooms cook for a minute to brown their bases lightly. Pour in the reserved mushroom water, or 2 tablespoons water, bring to a boil, and cover the pan tightly. Reduce heat to low, and simmer the mushrooms for 15 minutes. Stir the oyster sauce into the liquid in the pan, and baste the mushrooms lightly. Cover the pan for a moment longer, then transfer the mushrooms to a serving dish. If any juice is left in the pan, spoon a bit over each mushroom.

Serve with steamed rice.

Hungarian Veal Cutlet

1 veal cutlet (about 4 ounces), pounded thin
Seasoned flour for dredging
½ tablespoon butter or margarine
½ teaspoon paprika
1 small green onion or shallot, finely chopped
1 tablespoon dry white wine
⅛ cup beef stock (⅙ bouillon cube dissolved in 2 tablespoons water)
½ teaspoon lemon juice
1 tablespoon sour cream
¼ teaspoon dill, chopped fresh or dehydrated

Dredge cutlet in the seasoned flour and shake off any excess. In a skillet, sauté the cutlet in the butter, over medium heat, until golden brown on both sides. Remove from pan.

Using the same pan, add the paprika, onions, wine, stock, and lemon juice. Simmer and stir constantly for about 5 minutes, or until the sauce thickens slightly. Add the sour cream and mix well until heated through, but do not boil.

Pour the sauce over the veal, sprinkle with the dill and serve.

Veal Cutlet and Mushrooms

1 veal cutlet (about 4 ounces), pounded thin
Seasoned flour for dredging
1 tablespoon butter or margarine
2 fresh mushrooms, sliced
1 tablespoon dry white wine
1 tablespoon sour cream
$\frac{1}{4}$ bouillon cube dissolved in 1 tablespoon water
$\frac{1}{4}$ teaspoon cornstarch dissolved in $1\frac{1}{2}$ teaspoons water
1 teaspoon parsley, chopped fine

Dredge the cutlet in the flour, shaking off the excess. In a skillet, brown the meat in the butter, using a high heat, until lightly browned on each side. Lower the heat to medium and add the mushrooms. Stir in the wine, sour cream, and bouillon. Mix in the cornstarch mixture, and simmer for about 5 minutes until sauce is slightly thickened.

Pour the sauce over the meat and serve sprinkled with the chopped parsley.

Braised Veal Shank with Herbs

1 veal shank
2 tablespoons olive oil
$\frac{1}{4}$ teaspoon thyme, crushed
$\frac{1}{4}$ teaspoon celery seed
$\frac{1}{4}$ teaspoon onion powder
$\frac{1}{8}$ teaspoon garlic powder

⅛ teaspoon Lemon Pepper
3 sprigs of parsley, chopped (about ½ cup)
⅓ cup chicken broth
⅓ cup white wine
1 tablespoon tomato paste
1 potato, peeled and sliced in ¾-inch slices (optional)
3 to 4 ounces frozen green beans (optional)

Carefully cut the skin on the veal shank in several places (as you would cut the fat around a steak) to prevent the meat from popping out. Heat the oil in a 2- to 3-quart saucepan. Brown the veal slightly in the oil, then add the seasonings, broth, wine and tomato paste. Cover tightly and cook over low heat about 1 hour, until tender. Add more broth if necessary.

About 30 minutes before meat is cooked, add the potato and the frozen green beans.

The broth in the pan will thicken slightly as it cooks. Serve it over the shank and vegetables for a tasty one-dish meal.

Wiener Schnitzel

½ cup buttermilk
4 to 5 saltine crackers, crushed fine
1 veal chop or cutlet, boned
Pepper to taste
Olive oil or vegetable oil for frying

Pour buttermilk into a shallow dish. Place the finely crushed crackers on a piece of wax paper or a saucer. Pound the chop or cutlet with a meat mallet until it has spread to about half again its original size. Sprinkle with pepper. Dip first into the buttermilk and then into the crumbs. Set aside. Heat oil in a skillet, being careful not to let it burn. When oil is hot, gently ease the chop into the pan and sauté quickly, 10 minutes or less, until golden brown on each side.

This is good served with spaghetti and tomato sauce. If you put the veal on to cook at the same time you place the spaghetti in boiling water, both will be done about the same time.

Veal Paprika with Noodles

1 veal steak, boned, and cut into ¾-inch cubes
Seasoned flour for dredging
1½ teaspoons oil
1 teaspoon paprika
1 or 2 tablespoons chopped onions *or* ½ teaspoon onion powder
2 or 3 fresh mushrooms, sliced
2 tablespoons evaporated milk or half-and-half
2 tablespoons whole fresh milk
1 cup noodles
2 tablespoons butter or margarine
¼ teaspoon poppy seeds

Preheat oven to 300° F.

Dredge the veal in flour, shaking off the excess. In a skillet, sauté the meat in oil, until browned. Remove meat to small baking dish or casserole, and sprinkle with the paprika. Sauté the onion in the remaining oil until golden brown. Add the mushrooms, the evaporated milk, and the fresh milk, and stir to blend well. (If you use onion powder, do not sauté the onion powder, just add it to the milk and proceed.) Pour the sauce over the meat, cover the dish, and bake for about 45 minutes, or until the meat is tender.

About 20 minutes before meat is finished, start boiling the water for the noodles. When it is boiling rapidly, add the noodles and cook about 10 minutes, until tender. Drain. Serve the meat over the noodles, sprinkled with poppy seeds.

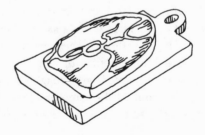

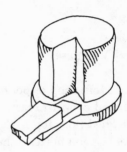

Veal Parmigiana

1 veal cutlet, or a piece of round steak, pounded thin
Salt and pepper to taste
1 egg, beaten
2 to 3 tablespoons bread crumbs or cracker crumbs
Grated Parmesan cheese to taste
Oil for sautéing
¼ cup tomato sauce
1 to 2 slices mozzarella cheese, sliced thin

Preheat oven to 350° F.

Pound meat thin, then season with salt and pepper. Dip it in the beaten egg, then into the bread or cracker crumbs, and finally, into the grated Parmesan cheese. (If you use pregrated cheese in a shaker jar, shake it over the cutlet on each side.) Pat cheese into the coating mixture.

In a skillet, sauté the meat in hot oil until golden brown. This will take just a few minutes because the meat is thin.

Place the meat in a shallow baking pan, pour the tomato sauce over it, top with thin slices of mozzarella cheese, and sprinkle a little grated Parmesan cheese over all. Bake in oven for about 15 minutes, or until the cheese melts and browns. Serve.

Veal Viennese

1 veal loin chop or pounded cutlet
Salt and pepper to taste
Seasoned flour for dredging
1 tablespoon butter or margarine
2 large fresh mushrooms, sliced thin
1 tablespoon dry white wine
1 tablespoon sour cream
¼ teaspoon meat extract *or* ¼ beef bouillon cube
1 tablespoon water
¼ teaspoon cornstarch dissolved in ¾ teaspoon water
¼ tablespoon finely chopped fresh parsley (optional)

Sprinkle the salt and pepper on the veal, then dredge in seasoned flour. Shake off excess flour.

Melt the butter in a heavy skillet, and sauté the veal over high heat for 2 to 3 minutes, until golden brown on each side.

Reduce heat and add the mushrooms, stirring to coat them with the butter. Let cook for 2 more minutes. Mix the wine, sour cream, meat extract, and 1 tablespoon water, and pour into the skillet. Stir once or twice to coat the meat and mushrooms. Let simmer while you mix the cornstarch and water to a thin, smooth consistency, then pour this into the pan. Stir briefly, then simmer for another 3 to 4 minutes. The liquid will thicken and reduce, coating the meat and the mushrooms. Remove from heat.

Pour the mushroom sauce over the meat, and sprinkle with the parsley. Serve.

Variation: Substitute a 3- to 4-ounce piece of round steak for the veal.

Veal Scallopini

1 veal cutlet, or slices from leg of veal, about ⅜ inch thick and 2 inches
   in diameter, *or* 3 to 4 ounces round steak, pounded to ¼ inch thin,
   and cut in strips
Parmesan cheese, grated
¼ cup butter, divided
¼ cup fresh mushrooms, finely sliced, *or* tiny mushroom caps, unsliced
Salt and cayenne pepper to taste
¼ cup beef stock, hot, and ¼ teaspoon meat extract *or* ½ beef bouillon
   cube dissolved in ½ cup hot water
¼ teaspoon butter or margarine
1 to 2 tablespoons white wine, preferably Marsala

Pound the meat thin and dip it in the cheese. In a skillet, sauté the
meat in 2 tablespoons butter until lightly browned on both sides.

In another pan, sauté the mushrooms in the remaining 2 tablespoons butter. Sprinkle lightly with salt and cayenne pepper.

When the meat is cooked, remove it to a serving dish and sprinkle
the cooked mushrooms over it. Pour the meat drippings, if any, the
beef stock and meat extract into the pan in which the mushrooms were
cooked, add ¼ teaspoon butter, and stir over a very low heat until the
sauce is well mixed. Increase the heat, and cook for 1 minute. While
the sauce is bubbling, add the wine and cook for only a second or two,
stirring, then pour the sauce over the meat and mushrooms.

Delicious served with spaghetti.

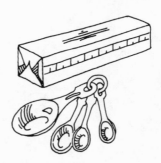

Osso Bucco *(Veal Shanks)*

3 veal shanks or 1 large shank cut into 3 rounds
1 teaspoon butter or margarine
2 teaspoons olive oil
$\frac{1}{2}$ medium carrot, grated
Salt and pepper to taste
2 tablespoons chopped celery *or* $\frac{1}{2}$ teaspoon celery seed
$\frac{1}{4}$ medium-sized onion, chopped, *or* $\frac{1}{2}$ teaspoon onion powder
Pinch each of rosemary, marjoram, and sage
1 teaspoon tomato paste
$\frac{1}{2}$ cup dry white wine, such as Chablis or Chenin Blanc
$\frac{1}{4}$ cup water or stock
$\frac{1}{2}$ teaspoon grated lemon rind, fresh or dried
1 tablespoon chopped parsley or parsley flakes
$\frac{1}{2}$ clove garlic, minced, *or* $\frac{1}{2}$ teaspoon garlic powder

In a skillet, brown veal shanks in butter and oil, then set them on the bone end. Add the carrot, salt, pepper, celery, onion, and herbs, and cover the pan. Simmer for 10 to 15 minutes, then blend in the tomato paste mixed with the wine. Stir into the juices in the pan, then add the water or stock. Cover and simmer over low heat for about $1\frac{1}{4}$ hours. Add liquid in small amounts if necessary.

Mix grated lemon peel, parsley, and garlic. When meat is tender, remove to a serving dish and sprinkle with this mixture. Serve with fluffy rice.

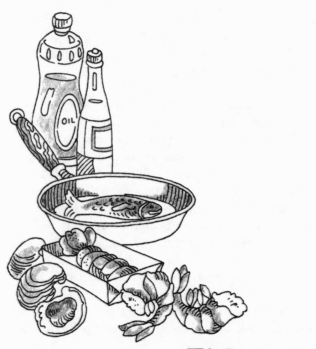

12

Fish and Seafood

Deep-Fried Fish and Chips

Batter for Fish

¼ cup flour
5 teaspoons water
1 tablespoon milk, water, or beer
1 tablespoon egg white, beaten stiff

1 potato, peeled
1 to 2 pieces firm white fish, about 3 inches square and 1 inch thick
Oil for frying
Salt to taste
Malt vinegar

To prepare batter, mix flour, water, and milk or beer in a wide, shallow dish until smooth and thick. Fold in the stiffly beaten egg white. Batter can be made ahead of time and allowed to sit, but it will become lighter as it does, so don't let it stand for too long.

Slice potato crosswise so you have roundish slices about ¼ inch thick. Dry the slices between two pieces of paper toweling. Set aside.

Wash pieces of fish, then pat dry between paper towels.

Heat oil in a skillet or wok. Oil should be about 2 inches deep in the center of wok or about 1 inch deep in skillet. When oil is hot (375° F.), dip the fish in the batter, making certain it is well coated on all sides. Fry fish until golden brown. Remove to a layer of paper towels. The fish may be kept in a warm oven until potatoes are ready.

Skim out any particles of batter that may be in the oil, then add potato slices, sliding them carefully into the hot oil. Fry to a light golden tan. Turn off fire and remove the chips with a slotted spoon. Drain on absorbent paper towels. Sprinkle lightly with salt.

Arrange fish and chips on a plate and dribble malt vinegar over the fish. Or place the vinegar in a small sauce dish and dip the fish into it as you eat it.

Oven-Baked Fish

½ cup flour, for dredging
Dash of Lemon Pepper
Dash of onion powder
Dash of garlic powder
1 whole small fish or fish fillet (trout, catfish, sole, sand dabs, cod)
2 tablespoons milk or water

Preheat oven to 400° F.

Put flour into a plastic or paper bag large enough to hold fish. Add the seasonings in the quantities you prefer. Moisten the fish in a small amount of milk or water, and drop it into the bag. Shake to coat the fish well. Place fish in a greased pan just large enough for it. (You may use a greased foil pan or pie tin.) Bake for about 20 minutes, then turn and bake another 10 to 15 minutes, until it is nicely browned and the meat is flaky.

Variation: If you prefer baked fish with a crunchy coating, roll the fish in egg and milk, then dredge in crushed corn flakes, crackers, or corn-meal instead of flour.

Stir-Fried Fish Fillets

½ pound boned, skinned white fish (such as sea bass, sole, pike)
1 teaspoon cornstarch
½ egg white (1 tablespoon)
1½ teaspoons Chinese rice wine or pale dry sherry
1 teaspoon salt or salt substitute
2 tablespoons peanut oil or other flavorless vegetable oil
½ teaspoon finely chopped ginger root *or* ¼ teaspoon powdered ginger
1 small green onion, including top, finely chopped, *or* ¼ teaspoon on-
    ion powder

Cut fish into bite-sized pieces. Place in a small bowl. Sprinkle with cornstarch and toss with a fork to coat well. Add egg white, wine, and salt, and mix until fish is well coated.

Place a small skillet or wok over high heat for a few seconds, then add oil and swirl it around the pan, letting it heat for another few seconds. (Reduce heat to moderate if oil begins to smoke.) When oil is heated, add the ginger and the green onion and stir into oil. If oil begins to smoke, reduce the heat—do not let ginger-onion mixture burn. Add the coated fish pieces and stir-fry gently until the fish is firm and white—about 1 minute. As soon as fish loses its transparent color and flakes easily, remove to a serving plate.

Serve with plain steamed rice and a green vegetable.

Tuna Croquettes

$\frac{1}{2}$ cup tuna, flaked, but undrained
$\frac{1}{2}$ egg (1 tablespoon egg white and $1\frac{1}{2}$ teaspoons egg yolk)
$\frac{1}{4}$ teaspoon onion powder
$\frac{1}{4}$ teaspoon sweet basil or thyme
$1\frac{1}{2}$ teaspoons flour
$\frac{1}{4}$ teaspoon bottled tempura sauce or soy sauce
$\frac{1}{2}$ teaspoon lemon juice
$\frac{1}{4}$ teaspoon Worcestershire sauce
2 or 3 saltine crackers, crushed fine
1 to 2 teaspoons butter, margarine, or oil for sautéing

Mix all ingredients, except cracker crumbs and butter, until well blended. Shape into one or more patties. If mixture is too moist, add a bit
more flour. The mixture should be quite soft. Place the patty (patties)
in the cracker crumbs, pressing gently but firmly enough for the
crumbs to adhere to the patty, then turn and crumb the other side.
Sauté the patties in the butter in a skillet over a moderately low heat
until nicely browned and crusty on each side—about 5 to 6 minutes per
side.

Serve plain or with a cheese sauce, catsup, chili sauce, tempura
sauce, or soy sauce.

To make traditional cone-shaped croquettes, form the mixture accordingly, then brown the croquettes, turning them as needed until
they are browned and crusty all over.

Lobster Cantonese

3 to 4 small lobster tails (or 2 large tails)
½ teaspoon soy sauce
½ teaspoon salt
⅛ teaspoon sugar
Dash ground pepper
1 green onion, about 3 inches long, finely chopped
1 tablespoon peanut or vegetable oil
½ teaspoon fermented black beans, chopped
½ teaspoon finely chopped garlic *or* ¼ teaspoon garlic powder
2 ounces lean ground pork *or* 1 pork chop, boned and minced
½ cup chicken stock, canned, fresh or made from bouillon cube dissolved in 1 cup water
1 tablespoon cornstarch dissolved in 1½ tablespoons cold water
1 egg, lightly beaten

Remove flesh from lobster shells and cut into bite-sized pieces. Mix soy sauce, salt, sugar, pepper, and green onion in a small dish.

Heat oil in a 10-inch skillet, then reduce the heat to moderate. Stir in black beans and garlic, making sure they don't burn. Add pork and cook until it loses its pink color. Add the soy sauce, salt, sugar, pepper, and green onion mixture, combining it well with the other ingredients in the pan. Add the lobster pieces. Cook, stirring, over a high heat for a minute or so. Pour in the chicken stock, cover pan, and cook for 5 minutes. Mix the cornstarch and pour it into the pan, stirring to distribute it well. As soon as the sauce thickens and becomes clear, slowly pour in the beaten egg, gently folding it in and lifting the contents from the sides of the pan with a fork or spoon. Remove pan from fire immediately. Serve.

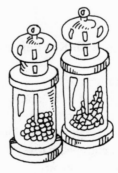

Indoor Clambake

1 to 2 pieces stewing chicken
Salt and pepper to taste
2 to 3 boiling onions or pearl onions (or ¼ medium regular onion)
1 medium potato or 3 small new potatoes, cut into chunks
Water
1 ear of corn, fresh or frozen
3 to 4 clams
2 to 3 lobster tails
4 tablespoons butter or margarine

Season chicken with salt and pepper. Place in a 3-quart kettle along with the onions and potatoes. Add water to cover. Bring to a boil over medium heat. Cover kettle, lower heat, and simmer for 30 minutes.

If using fresh corn, remove corn silk but leave the husk intact. Place it in pot on top of chicken and vegetables; cover, and simmer another 30 minutes. If using frozen corn, add it to the pot 10 to 15 minutes before end of cooking.

If using fresh clams, scrub the shells well. If using canned clams in the shell, open and drain the clams, reserving the juice for later. Put clams and lobster tails into the pot. Cover and let steam for 15 minutes more, until lobster tails have turned a coral color.

Melt butter in a saucepan. Warm reserved clam juice, if any.

Arrange ingredients on a plate. Pour melted butter into a small dipping dish and the clam juice into another dipping dish. Dip lobster, potato, and corn into the butter or margarine, and the clams into the juice. Or, if you prefer, pour the butter or margarine and the clam juice over all the items.

Sea Scallops with Red Peppers

4 ounces scallops
1 teaspoon butter or margarine
¼ teaspoon garlic powder
1 teaspoon minced green onions *or* ½ teaspoon onion powder
2 teaspoons chopped parsley
Pinch of dried tarragon

Dash of black pepper

1 tablespoon chopped red (or green) bell pepper, cored and seeded

1 tablespoon chicken broth, fresh, canned or made from a crushed
    piece of bouillon cube and 1 cup water

Wash the scallops and pat dry. Melt butter in a saucepan and add the
garlic, green onions, parsley, tarragon, and black pepper. When seasonings are well mixed with the butter, add the chopped pepper. Cook 2 to
3 minutes until the peppers are just tender (not too soft), and then add
the chicken broth. Add scallops and toss in pan until they are just
cooked and lightly browned, about 2 to 3 minutes per side. Do not
overcook scallops—they become tough.

Serve scallops with the sauce poured over them.

Alternate method: Prepare sauce, place the scallops in a shallow dish,
and pour the sauce over them. Then bake in a 450° F. oven for 8 to 12
minutes, until done.

Coquilles Saint-Jacques à la Parisienne

$\frac{1}{2}$ cup fresh or canned chicken stock, skimmed, *or* 1 bouillon cube dis-
    solved in $\frac{1}{2}$ cup hot water

$\frac{1}{2}$ cup dry white wine

1 green onion or shallot, sliced

1 celery stalk with leaves, cut into 2-inch pieces

1 sprig parsley, minced

$\frac{1}{3}$ bay leaf

3 whole peppercorns

6 to 8 scallops, cut into $\frac{1}{2}$-inch slices

5 to 6 fresh mushrooms, sliced, *or* $\frac{1}{2}$ cup canned button mushrooms

Preheat oven to 375° F.

In a heavy 1-quart saucepan, over a high flame, bring to a boil the
stock, wine, green onion, celery, parsley, bay leaf, and peppercorns.
Reduce heat and simmer, uncovered, for 20 minutes. You may use this
court bouillon unstrained, or, if you prefer, strain it through a sieve
into a skillet.

Add scallops and mushrooms to court bouillon, cover, and simmer
for 5 minutes. Remove scallops and mushrooms to a bowl, then boil
the liquid until it reduces to about half.

Sauce Parisienne

1⅓ tablespoons butter or margarine
1¼ tablespoons flour
¼ cup milk
1 egg yolk (or 1 whole egg)
3 tablespoons heavy cream
Few drops lemon juice
Salt, white pepper to taste
3 tablespoons grated imported Swiss or Parmesan cheese

Melt butter in saucepan over moderate heat. When the foam subsides, remove from heat and stir in the flour until smooth. Return to low heat and, stirring constantly, cook for a minute or two. Do not let it brown. Remove from heat and slowly pour in the reduced court bouillon and the milk. Cook over high heat, stirring constantly. When it thickens and comes to a boil, reduce heat and let simmer for 1 minute. Mix egg yolk and cream together in a small bowl. Stir a little of the hot sauce into it. Add a bit more sauce, then stir this sauce mixture into the remaining sauce in the pan. Bring to a boil, stirring constantly, and boil for half a minute. Remove from heat, and season with lemon juice, salt, and pepper. The sauce should coat a spoon fairly thickly. If it is too thick, thin with cream.

Pour a bit of the sauce directly into a baking dish. Place the scallops and mushrooms on top of the sauce. Pour the remaining sauce over the scallops and mushrooms, then add the cheese. Bake in the upper third of the oven for 10 to 15 minutes until sauce bubbles, then slide the dish under the broiler for a few seconds to brown the top, if desired.

Serve with a small green salad and French bread for an elegant (but inexpensive) dinner.

Red and White Sea Scallops

The surprise element in this dish is pork kidney, an ingredient not often used in cooking—unfortunately so, since it is amazingly tender and sweet. Its mild flavor goes well with the scallops. This dish is easier to make than it looks. You can prepare it and have dinner ready in 30 minutes or less.

6 to 8 scallops
1 teaspoon pale dry sherry or Chinese rice wine
Dash of salt
1 pork kidney
1 teaspoon finely chopped fresh ginger root
1 green onion, finely sliced
2 teaspoons soy sauce
$\frac{1}{4}$ teaspoon sugar
$\frac{1}{2}$ teaspoon cornstarch dissolved in 1 teaspoon water or chicken stock
4 teaspoons peanut oil (or other vegetable oil), divided

Gather all ingredients together. Slice the scallops $\frac{1}{4}$ inch thick, then set them near the wine and salt—you'll use these three together first.

Next, slice the kidney in half lengthwise, and lay the flat sides down on the cutting board. Make crisscross slashes across the top of each piece, on a diagonal, then cut these two pieces into quarters or bite-sized pieces. Set them aside, together with the ginger root, green onion, soy sauce, and sugar.

Mix the cornstarch, and set it aside.

In a 10-inch skillet, heat 2 teaspoons of oil. Add the scallops, lower the heat to moderate, and stir for 1 minute or until the scallops turn white, but not too firm. Add wine and salt, stir well, then remove scallops and juices from pan and reserve.

Put in the 2 remaining teaspoons of oil, heat for about 30 seconds, and add the ginger and green onion. Stir for several seconds, then add the kidney pieces. Stir-fry briefly over high heat until their edges begin to curl, then add the soy sauce and sugar. Return the scallops and juices to the pan and stir.

Stir cornstarch mixture quickly to blend it, then add to the pan. Stir the mixture until all the pieces are coated with a clear glaze. This will take only a few seconds. Remove from pan immediately and serve.

For an excellent accompaniment, serve with steamed rice and asparagus.

Crab Meat and Cucumber Salad

$\frac{1}{8}$ pound fresh crab meat *or* half a $7\frac{1}{2}$-ounce can of crab meat
2-inch piece of peeled cucumber, seeds removed
$1\frac{1}{2}$ teaspoons white vinegar
$1\frac{1}{2}$ teaspoons soy sauce
$\frac{1}{4}$ teaspoon sugar
Dash of ground white or black pepper
$\frac{3}{4}$ teaspoon sesame seed oil

Remove any bits of shell in the crab meat. Shred cucumber coarsely, or cut into thin slices, then crosscut slices into small strips, removing the seeds.

In a small bowl, mix remaining ingredients, then add the cucumber and crab meat, tossing together so that they are well coated with the dressing.

Chill slightly, no more than 45 minutes, and serve.

Deep-Fried Shrimp and Vegetables

$\frac{1}{2}$ egg yolk (1$\frac{1}{2}$ teaspoons)
2 tablespoons ice-cold water
Pinch of baking powder
4 tablespoons plus 1 teaspoon flour, divided
$\frac{1}{4}$ small carrot, shredded (about 2 tablespoons)
$\frac{3}{4}$ teaspoon scraped fresh ginger *or* diced preserved ginger, *or* $\frac{1}{8}$ to $\frac{1}{4}$
teaspoon powdered ginger
$\frac{1}{3}$ cup fresh or frozen shrimp, diced in $\frac{1}{4}$-inch pieces
$\frac{1}{8}$ cup shelled green peas
Oil for frying
Garnishes: bottled tempura sauce or soy sauce, fresh or powdered
ginger

Mix egg yolk, water, and baking powder. Add 4 tablespoons plus 1 teaspoon flour and stir until well blended. Into this batter, stir remaining ingredients.

Place $\frac{1}{4}$ inch oil in a wok, skillet, or tempura pan, and heat.

Mix the vegetables with the batter until they are well coated. Shape into two or more patties about $\frac{1}{2}$ inch thick. A good way to do this is to drop spoonfuls of batter onto squares of wax paper, then shape the patty and set aside.

When oil is hot, dip a wide spatula into it, then turn the patty onto the oiled spatula and slip it carefully into the batter. Repeat with other patties. Fry until golden brown, then turn and fry the other side. Drain on paper towels.

Serve on a bed of boiled or steamed rice, placing the patties on top of each other. Pour $\frac{1}{8}$ to $\frac{1}{4}$ cup of the bottled tempura sauce over the patties, or use soy sauce. Sprinkle a little powdered ginger on the top.

Note: Put the rice on to cook when you begin to prepare the batter— both will be done about the same time.

Phoenix-Tailed Shrimp

$\frac{1}{2}$ pound raw shrimp
$1\frac{1}{2}$ teaspoons rice wine or pale dry sherry
$\frac{1}{2}$ teaspoon salt
$\frac{1}{16}$ teaspoon white or black pepper
$\frac{3}{4}$ cup flour, sifted
$\frac{1}{2}$ cup water
$\frac{1}{2}$ tablespoon double-acting baking powder
Oil for deep-frying
Sauce for dipping (recipe follows)

Peel shrimp, leaving the tails on, then devein and wash them. Pat dry with paper towels. On the underside (inner curve) of each shrimp, cut three-quarters of the way through, going the full length of the shrimp. Then, flatten each shrimp, using a plate, a heavy knife, or the weight of your hand. Mix the wine, salt, and pepper. Sprinkle the cut sides of the shrimp with this mixture, then set aside.

Prepare a batter by mixing the flour and water to a smooth paste. Add the baking powder, and stir again. Set aside, near the shrimp.

Place enough oil in a saucepan or deep-fryer to cover the shrimp, about $1\frac{1}{2}$ inches to 2 inches deep. Heat oil until it registers 375° F. on a deep-frying thermometer. Holding the shrimp by the tails, dip them one at a time into the batter, then carefully drop them into the oil. Do not crowd the pan—fry about 4 at a time, depending on the size of the shrimp and the pan. Cook 2 to 3 minutes, turning them once or twice, until they are golden brown. Drain on paper towels.

Note: The shrimp can also be deep-fried without cutting and flattening them. To prevent them from curling, weave them onto a toothpick, placing one end of the shrimp at either end of the toothpick. When fried, remove the toothpick.

Mustard Sauce for Dipping

Pour a small amount of catsup into a small sauce dish. In another small dish, mix a pinch of dry hot mustard with several drops of water until it becomes a smooth paste, then add this to the catsup, or place it just to the side of the catsup in the same dish. Another sauce suggestion: prepared horseradish or the powdered horseradish available in Oriental markets and some grocery stores.

Shrimp with Cantonese Sauce

6 to 8 small raw shrimp
2 tablespoons peanut oil or other vegetable oil, divided
1 teaspoon Chinese rice wine or pale dry sherry
$\frac{1}{2}$ teaspoon fermented black beans, chopped
$\frac{1}{4}$ teaspoon finely chopped garlic *or* $\frac{1}{8}$ teaspoon garlic powder
2 ounces lean pork, ground or finely minced
1 teaspoon soy sauce
Dash of salt and pepper
Pinch of sugar
1 small green onion, finely chopped
$\frac{1}{4}$ cup chicken stock, fresh, canned, or made from a bouillon cube dissolved in $\frac{1}{4}$ cup water
$\frac{1}{2}$ tablespoon cornstarch dissolved in 1 tablespoon water or cold chicken stock
1 egg, lightly beaten

Shell, devein and wash the shrimp. Pat dry with paper towels. Set out all remaining ingredients.

Heat 1 tablespoon oil in a skillet for a few seconds. If oil begins to smoke, lower the heat. Drop in the shrimp and stir for a minute or so, until they turn pink. Add the wine, stir once or twice, then turn the shrimp and wine out onto a plate.

Add the remaining oil to the pan. While it heats, stir in the fermented black beans and the garlic. Add the pork, stirring until it loses its pink color. Then add the soy sauce, salt, pepper, sugar, green onion, shrimp, and chicken stock. Cover and bring to a boil. Mix the cornstarch with water and add, stirring, until the sauce thickens and becomes clear. Pour in the egg in a slow stream. As you do so, using a large spoon, lift the contents of the pan gently from the sides so that the egg blends with the other ingredients without any further cooking. Remove to a plate and serve.

Especially good with rice and Chinese pea pods or snow peas, or asparagus, green peas, or string beans.

Deep-Fried Shrimp with Sweet and Sour Sauce

Sweet and Sour Sauce

1 teaspoon cornstarch
1 tablespoon plus 2⅓ teaspoons water
1 tablespoon plus 1 teaspoon distilled white vinegar
1⅓ teaspoons dark brown sugar

6 to 8 medium-sized shrimp (about ¼ pound), canned, fresh, or frozen, shells removed

To prepare the sauce, dissolve the cornstarch in cold water in a small saucepan. Add vinegar and brown sugar and cook over moderate heat, stirring, until the sauce thickens and becomes transparent. Remove from heat and set the pan aside, covered, to keep the sauce warm.

Batter

2 tablespoons flour
2 tablespoons warm water
1 teaspoon vegetable oil
Salt and pepper to taste
1 egg white, beaten stiff
Oil for deep-frying

Prepare the batter by mixing flour, warm water, oil, salt, and pepper. Fold in the stiffly beaten egg white.

Clean and devein the shrimp.

Into a skillet, saucepan, or wok, pour oil to a depth of ½ inch to ¾ inch, and heat until a light haze forms. Dip the shrimp into the batter, coating it heavily, then carefully drop the shrimp into the hot oil, taking care that the shrimp do not touch and the pan is not crowded. Fry until golden brown and crisp on both sides. Drain on paper towels.

Reheat the sauce if it has cooled. Put the shrimp on a plate, and pour the sauce over them, or serve separately, placing the sauce in a small dish for dipping. The shrimp may also be put into the sauce in the pan and coated, then removed to a plate.

13

Vegetables

BASIC BUTTERED VEGETABLES

Most vegetables are very good when served simply with a dressing of butter, salt, and pepper. To achieve this, simply cook the vegetables either by boiling in water or by steaming. To boil vegetables, clean, trim, and slice as desired. Bring to boil enough water to cover; add a dash of salt if desired. Add vegetables, return to the boil, lower heat, and simmer just until tender.

There are two ways to steam vegetables. You can use either a heavy, waterless-cooking-type pan with a close-fitting cover, and add a tablespoon of water (or less, depending on the water content of the vegetable), or you can use a steaming tray or basket inserted into a larger pan. Fill the pan with about ½ cup water and place the vegetables in the steaming tray. In either method, bring the water to a boil, lower the flame as much as possible (sometimes sliding the pan halfway off the heat), cover the pan, and cook for a few minutes. Cooking time varies from about 5 or 6 minutes for fresh spinach to about 20 minutes for tougher vegetables, such as carrots or turnips.

When the vegetable is tender, drain the water, add a pat of butter or margárine, and serve. You may add a dash of salt and pepper, but do try the vegetable first without salt, especially if you cook by the steaming method.

Vegetables that can be cooked by boiling or steaming are, among others, asparagus, green beans, lima beans, corn, carrots, potatoes, peas, cauliflower, zucchini, broccoli, Brussels sprouts, sweet potatoes, yams, and any other garden vegetable, whether fresh or frozen.

For variety, instead of the butter dressing you can serve a cream or cheese sauce. The sauce is added after the vegetables are cooked, either mixing it with the vegetables in the pan or pouring it over the vegetable at serving time.

Marinated Vegetables

This recipe is enough for 4 to 5 portions, which enables you to prepare vegetables ahead for several one-serving dinners or for lunch. You can prepare a variety of vegetables at once and eat a different one each day, or you can have a portion of all at one meal. It is advisable, however, to marinate only the amount of vegetables you will consume within a week, since after that time they begin to lose their firm texture and are not as palatable. Save the marinade, and cook a few more vegetables later on. This marinade makes about 2½ cups.

Marinade

1½ cups chicken stock, fresh or canned
½ cup dry white wine
½ cup olive oil
¼ cup lemon juice
3 parsley sprigs
1 large garlic clove, chopped
¼ teaspoon dried thyme
5 peppercorns
½ teaspoon salt

Stir the ingredients together in a 2- to 3-quart heavy saucepan. Bring to a boil, partially cover the pan, and simmer slowly for 45 minutes. Strain the marinade through a fine sieve into a large bowl, pressing the ingredients with the back of a spoon to squeeze out their juices before discarding them. (Or, you may liquefy them in your blender.) Return the marinade to the saucepan, and taste for seasoning. It should have a strong flavor to be effective.

Vegetables

3 to 4 white onions, 1 inch in diameter, peeled
1 to 2 small zucchini, unpeeled, sliced 1 inch thick
1 to 2 small yellow squash, unpeeled, sliced 1 inch thick
1 green pepper, cored and seeded, and cut lengthwise into $\frac{1}{2}$-inch strips
$\frac{1}{4}$ pound (8 to 10) whole green string beans, trimmed

The following may be added or substituted as desired:

1 to 2 leeks, chopped
1 to 2 cucumbers, peeled, sliced 1 inch thick
1 red bell pepper, cored, seeded, and cut in strips
2 to 3 artichoke hearts
3 to 4 fresh mushrooms, washed and sliced
2 to 3 celery hearts

Bring the marinade to a boil. Add the onions. Cover and cook over moderate heat for 20 to 30 minutes, or until just tender when pierced with the tip of a sharp knife. With a slotted spoon, remove the onions to a dish or bowl, with a tight-fitting cover.

Add the slices of zucchini and yellow squash to the simmering marinade. Cook slowly, uncovered, for 10 to 15 minutes, or until barely done, then put them in the same dish as the onions.

Add the green pepper strips and string beans. Cook slowly, uncovered, for 8 to 10 minutes, or until just tender. Add them to the other vegetables.

Note: Do *not* overcook the vegetables, because they soften as they cool and marinate.

Taste and season the marinade, then pour it over the vegetables, making sure they are all at least partly covered with the hot marinade. Cool. Cover the bowl, dish, or jar securely, and place it in the refrigerator. Serve vegetables cold, a few at a time, as desired.

This recipe makes a nice addition to a picnic or buffet dinner. It also provides bright, zesty appetizers for a cocktail party or predinner drinks. For such events, arrange the marinated vegetables decoratively on a large serving dish or a silver tray, with plenty of toothpicks. Garnish with lemon slices and parsley. They can also be served in individual dishes on a lazy Susan tray, with a bit of the extra marinade offered in the center bowl, for dipping.

Quick Vegetable Medley

This is a good dish for a hot summer night when you would rather not be in the kitchen. It is nourishing, economical, easy, and quick.

1 tablespoon olive oil
1 medium zucchini, sliced about ¼ inch thick
½ medium green pepper, cored, seeded, and cut into cubes
2 or 3 fresh mushrooms, diced or cubed
1 medium tomato, chopped into pieces about ¾ inch square
½ cup coarsely grated Swiss cheese
Pinch of basil
Pinch of tarragon
Dash of Lemon Pepper (optional)

Heat the oil in a 1-quart saucepan or skillet. Add the zucchini and green pepper and sauté for a few minutes, until not quite tender. Add the mushrooms and cook another 2 or 3 minutes. Add the tomato cubes, simmer for 2 more minutes, then add the cheese and herbs. Mix them into the vegetables and cook over low heat until cheese is melted. Serve garnished with Lemon Pepper if desired.

Serve with French-fried round steak (pounded and dredged in flour) for a nice dinner that will take about 20 minutes to prepare from start to finish.

Creamed Asparagus

4 to 8 stalks fresh asparagus, cut in bite-sized pieces
¼ cup water (approximately)
1 tablespoon butter or margarine
¼ cup milk or cream (approximately)
Salt and pepper to taste

Place asparagus bits and water in a small, heavy saucepan with a tightly fitting lid. Bring water to a boil, then lower flame to simmer. Cook about 10 to 12 minutes, until pieces are tender.

Do not drain the liquid from the pan. Add the butter and milk. Season with salt and pepper. Heat only long enough to warm the milk. Serve.

Chinese Asparagus

4 to 6 stalks fresh asparagus
2 water chestnuts
2 to 3 fresh mushrooms, 1-inch size *or* 8 to 12 canned button mush-
    rooms
Oil, to lightly cover bottom of pan
Salt and pepper to taste

Break off stem ends of asparagus stalks. Peel ends down to the tender
part. Cut stalks and peeled ends into 1-inch pieces, cutting on the diagonal. Slice the water chestnuts and mushrooms into $\frac{1}{4}$-inch slices. (If
using canned button mushrooms, do not slice.) Heat oil in skillet or
wok. When it is very hot, place the asparagus, water chestnuts, and
mushrooms in the oil and cook, stirring constantly, for 4 to 5 minutes
or until barely tender—still crisp and bright colored. Season to taste
and serve with fluffy boiled rice and fresh tomato slices.

Green Beans with Sour Cream Sauce

$\frac{1}{2}$ cup green beans, trimmed and cut in 1-inch pieces
Water for cooking
$\frac{1}{8}$ teaspoon onion powder
$\frac{1}{8}$ teaspoon garlic powder
2 teaspoons paprika
$\frac{1}{4}$ cup commercial sour cream
Pepper to taste

Cook green beans in small amount of water in a tightly covered saucepan until tender, about 20 minutes. Drain.

Add the onion powder, garlic powder, paprika, sour cream, and
pepper to the beans in the pan, and stir well to mix together. Simmer
for a few seconds until the sour cream is hot and all ingredients are
well blended, but do not boil. Serve.

Green Beans and Water Chestnuts

½ cup green beans, fresh or frozen and thawed
1 scant tablespoon peanut oil or vegetable oil
¼ teaspoon sugar
1 or 2 water chestnuts cut into ¼-inch slices
1 tablespoon chicken stock, fresh, canned or made by dissolving a
    bouillon cube in 1 cup water
¼ teaspoon cornstarch dissolved in a small amount of cold water or
    stock

Cut the green beans into pieces, 1 inch to 2 inches long. Heat the oil in
a skillet or wok. Drop in the string beans and stir-fry for about 3 minutes, or not quite 2 minutes if using thawed frozen beans. Add the sugar, water chestnuts, and chicken stock, and stir a couple of times.
Cover the pan and cook for 2 to 3 minutes, until the beans are tender
yet crisp. Stir the cornstarch mixture again to recombine it and add to
the pan. Cook, stirring, until the beans and water chestnuts are coated
with a light, clear glaze.

Green Beans with Bell Peppers

½ cup frozen or fresh green beans (about ¼ pound), stringed and cut
    into any size desired
⅛ teaspoon tarragon, crushed
1½ to 2 tablespoons water
1 small red bell pepper, cut into 1-inch squares

Put cut beans, tarragon, and water into a small saucepan. Bring to a fast
simmer, and cover pan tightly. Lower heat to very lowest level, and
cook beans for about 10 minutes without stirring. Add the pepper
pieces, cover the pan, and simmer for another 5 to 6 minutes or until
the peppers and beans are tender but still retain some crispness. Drain
off any liquid and serve.

   If you use frozen green beans, add less water (about 1 tablespoon)
because of the moisture already in the beans.

Tarragon Beans with Fresh Tomato

$\frac{1}{2}$ cup fresh or frozen green beans, cut into 1-inch pieces
Water for cooking
$\frac{1}{2}$ tablespoon butter or margarine
$\frac{1}{4}$ teaspoon tarragon leaves, crushed
$\frac{1}{2}$ teaspoon Lemon Pepper
1 small tomato (or half a large or medium one), cubed

If using fresh green beans, snap off the ends and string them, then cut into pieces. (If using frozen beans, this step is unnecessary.)

Cook the beans about 15 minutes in a small amount of water, in a pan with a tight-fitting lid. When the beans are tender, drain them. Add the butter, tarragon, Lemon Pepper, and cubed tomato. Cover the pan and return it to a low heat to melt the butter and heat the tomato slightly—about 3 to 5 minutes. Stir frequently or shake the pan to prevent burning. Serve.

Bean Sprouts, Mushrooms, and Peas

2 large mushrooms, sliced
2 teaspoons oil
1 cup bean sprouts
$\frac{1}{2}$ cup green peas
1 teaspoon sesame seeds
1 teaspoon soy sauce
Dash of onion powder
Dash of black pepper, preferably freshly ground

In a skillet, sauté the mushrooms in the oil for about 3 minutes. Add the bean sprouts, peas, sesame seeds, soy sauce, and a dash each of onion powder and pepper. Stir gently to mix the vegetables well but not break them. Cover the pan and cook 2 to 3 minutes more. Serve.

Harvard Beets

1 small can beets, whole, diced, sliced, or julienne strips (retain juice)
1 teaspoon sugar
1 teaspoon vinegar
½ teaspoon butter or margarine
1 teaspoon cornstarch dissolved in 2 teaspoons water or beet juice

Drain beet juice into saucepan. Add sugar and vinegar and stir to dissolve sugar. Bring to a hard simmer and add butter. Taste sauce; it should be a mellow blend of the sugar and vinegar. If either flavor is more pronounced, add a bit more of the other to balance, and stir. Add the cornstarch mixed with water and stir until sauce thickens. Add beets and stir to coat beets. Simmer only long enough to heat beets thoroughly. Serve.

Broccoli Roman Style

2 stalks fresh broccoli, washed
1 tablespoon olive oil
Dash of freshly ground pepper
¼ cup dry white wine
Grated Parmesan cheese

Use the broccoli stalks full size or cut into bite-sized pieces. In a skillet, sauté in oil about 5 minutes. Sprinkle lightly with pepper. Pour in wine, lower heat, cover pan tightly, and simmer until tender, 10 to 15 minutes. Sprinkle with Parmesan cheese before serving.

Stir-Fried Broccoli

1 to 2 tablespoons peanut oil or other flavorless vegetable oil
3 stalks fresh broccoli, washed and cut into bite-sized pieces
Dash of salt
Dash of sugar
1 tablespoon chicken stock, fresh, canned, or made by dissolving granulated chicken stock or bouillon cube in 1 cup water
$\frac{1}{4}$ teaspoon cornstarch dissolved in a small amount of cold chicken
stock or water

Heat the oil in a skillet for several seconds. Lower the heat to moderate
so the oil won't smoke. Drop in the broccoli stalks and stir-fry for a
minute or so. Drop in the broccoli florets, and stir-fry for another minute, coating all the pieces in the oil. Sprinkle in the salt and sugar, then
add the chicken stock, stirring for several seconds. Cover the pan and
cook for 2 to 3 minutes, until the broccoli is tender but still crisp. Stir
the cornstarch mixture to recombine it, then pour it into the pan. Stir
until the broccoli is coated with a light, clear glaze. Serve.

Creamed Chinese Cabbage

$\frac{1}{4}$ pound celery cabbage (Chinese cabbage) or bok choy
1 rounded teaspoon cornstarch
1 tablespoon cold milk
$\frac{1}{2}$ teaspoon peanut oil or flavorless vegetable oil
$\frac{1}{4}$ teaspoon salt
Pinch of sugar
$\frac{1}{4}$ cup chicken stock, fresh or canned
$\frac{1}{4}$ cup cooked ham, finely chopped (optional)

Separate the cabbage stalks, wash and trim them, then cut into pieces:
For bok choy, cut crosswise into 1-inch pieces; for celery cabbage, cut
into 1-inch by 2-inch pieces. Dissolve the cornstarch in the cold milk.

Heat the oil in a skillet. If it begins to smoke, lower the heat to moderate. Add the cabbage and stir-fry for about 1 minute, or until the cabbage pieces are coated with the oil. Sprinkle in the salt and sugar, then pour in the chicken stock and stir well. Bring to a boil and cover the pan. Reduce the heat to low and simmer, without stirring, for 10 minutes, or until tender. With a slotted spoon, remove the cabbage to a serving dish. Then raise the heat, bringing the liquid to a boil. Mix the cornstarch to recombine it, and stir it into the liquid, continuing to stir until the sauce thickens. Pour the sauce over the cabbage, and sprinkle with chopped ham if desired.

Stir-Fried Spiced Cabbage

¼ pound Chinese cabbage (celery cabbage), bok choy, or regular green
   cabbage
½ tablespoon sugar
½ tablespoon white vinegar
¼ scant teaspoon soy sauce
Dash of salt to taste
Few grains cayenne pepper to taste
¼ tablespoon peanut oil or flavorless vegetable oil

Separate cabbage into stalks or leaves, wash and trim, and cut into pieces 1 inch by 1½ inches. In a cup or small bowl, combine the sugar, vinegar, soy sauce, salt, and cayenne pepper, and mix well.

Pour the oil into a heated skillet, and heat for a few seconds. Lower the heat to moderate, and add the cabbage. Stir-fry for 2 to 3 minutes, being sure to coat all the cabbage with the oil. Remove the pan from the heat and stir in the soy-vinegar-sugar combination.

This is good hot, lukewarm, cool, and even chilled.

Dilled Red Cabbage

¼ small head red cabbage, sliced thin
¼ teaspoon poppy seed
⅛ teaspoon dillweed
Sour cream

Cook cabbage by steam method (p. 125) 5 to 10 minutes just until tender but still crisp. Add poppy seed and dill and toss. Garnish with sour cream.

Or cook cabbage, poppy seed, and dillweed in a small amount of water until cabbage is tender crisp. Drain and garnish with sour cream.

Orange-Parsley Carrots

¾ cup raw carrot, finely sliced
¼ cup orange juice
½ cup fresh parsley, chopped
1 teaspoon butter or margarine

Place all ingredients in a 1-quart saucepan. Bring to a boil and stir well. Cover the pan, reduce heat, and cook over a very low heat (so steam does not escape) until the carrots are tender, about 20 minutes. Serve carrots with sauce.

Note: If a lot of liquid is left in the pan, turn the heat to high and, stirring, boil until the liquid is reduced to the desired amount.

Glazed Carrots

1 or 2 carrots, scrubbed or peeled
3 tablespoons water or stock
1 tablespoon brown sugar
1 tablespoon butter or margarine
1 teaspoon chopped parsley

Cut carrots crosswise in ¼-inch slices. Or, if you prefer, make julienne strips: slice each carrot lengthwise into ¼-inch strips, then cut these strips crosswise into ¼-inch strips, and finally, cut all of these strips into pieces 1½ inches to 2 inches long.

Put all ingredients except the parsley into a saucepan. Bring the liquid to a simmer. Cover the pan tightly, and cook over low heat 15 to 20 minutes, until the carrots are tender but still firm. Shake the pan several times to coat the carrots with the liquid. Remove the carrots, and if the liquid is not yet a brown, syrupy glaze, raise the heat and continue cooking to reduce the quantity. Return the carrots to the liquid and stir until they are well coated with the glaze or pour the syrup over the carrots on your plate. Sprinkle with chopped parsley and serve.

Pineapple Carrots

3 to 4 small carrots, sliced thin on a diagonal
3 to 4 tablespoons pineapple juice
2 teaspoons butter or margarine
2 teaspoons brown sugar, firmly packed

In a tightly covered pan over low heat, cook the carrots in the pineapple juice until tender but still firm, about 15 to 20 minutes. Uncover, add the butter and brown sugar. Stir the carrots until they are well coated with the butter-sugar mixture and the sugar has melted. If there is too much juice, increase the heat and boil, uncovered, to reduce the liquid. Serve hot.

Cauliflower in Cheese Sauce

$\frac{1}{4}$ to $\frac{1}{2}$ head fresh cauliflower, as desired
Water for cooking
$\frac{1}{2}$ tablespoon butter or margarine
$\frac{1}{2}$ tablespoon flour
$\frac{1}{2}$ cup milk
$\frac{1}{4}$ cup diced or slivered mild Cheddar cheese
Salt and pepper to taste

Wash portion of cauliflower to be used. Trim off stem end and slice stem piece into $\frac{1}{4}$-inch slices. Place the leaves (if any) in bottom of saucepan. Add the stem pieces, then break florets into pieces into the pan. Add enough water to steam—about 1 tablespoon. Bring to a boil, lower heat, cover pan, and simmer about 15 minutes, or until cauliflower is just tender.

Meanwhile, prepare the sauce. In a small saucepan, melt the butter, add the flour, and stir well to moisten all the flour. Add the milk, a little at a time, stirring until mixture becomes smooth. Add the cheese and stir constantly until sauce thickens. Season to taste with salt and pepper, then add cooked and drained cauliflower. Stir gently to coat the cauliflower thoroughly with the sauce. Serve. Pour any extra sauce over the cauliflower.

Alternate one-pan method: After cauliflower has cooked, drain, and remove cauliflower to a separate dish. In the same pan, prepare the cheese sauce, then return the cauliflower to the sauce, stir to coat the cauliflower, and serve.

Variation: Reserve cooking liquid after draining from cauliflower. Use as liquid for making cheese sauce, adding enough milk to make $\frac{1}{2}$ cup liquid.

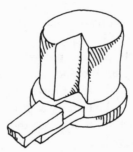

Cauliflower with Buttered Crumbs

¼ to ½ head fresh cauliflower, as desired
Water for cooking
3 tablespoons butter or margarine
3 tablespoons fine bread crumbs

Wash the portion of cauliflower to be used. Trim off stem end. Slice stem pieces into ¼-inch slices. Place the leaves (if any) in bottom of saucepan. Add the stems, then break cauliflower into pieces and add to pan. Add enough water to steam—about ¼ tablespoon. Bring to a boil, lower heat, cover the pan, and simmer about 15 minutes, or until cauliflower is barely tender. Drain.

In a small saucepan or skillet, melt the butter. Add the crumbs, stirring constantly to lightly brown them. Add the crumbs to the cauliflower and stir to coat the pieces, or sprinkle crumbs over cauliflower on a serving plate.

Alternate method: After draining the cauliflower, add the butter and crumbs to the cauliflower still in the pan, stir until butter is melted, then serve.

Sautéed Mushrooms

3 or 4 large mushrooms
1 to 2 teaspoons butter or margarine

With a damp cloth or paper towel wipe mushrooms clean, or rinse under running water (do not soak in water). Trim off lower stem ends and discard. Slice remaining stems and mushroom caps about ⅜ inch thick. Heat butter in a skillet or saucepan until bubbly, add mushrooms, and stir well, tossing pieces to coat in the butter. Cook over medium heat until lightly browned and somewhat reduced in size. Stir and toss frequently. When tender, remove from pan and serve. Excellent served over cooked meat or as a separate vegetable dish.

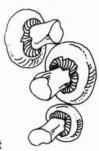

Creamed Mushrooms on Toast

This makes a nice, light dinner, an excellent breakfast, or a warm, delightful lunch. Creamed mushrooms are also excellent served over a hamburger patty or a piece of steak.

2 cups sliced mushrooms (about 4   2-inch-size mushrooms)
1 to 2 teaspoons butter or margarine
2 slices white bread
½ tablespoon flour
¼ to ½ cup milk
Salt and pepper to taste (optional)

Wipe mushrooms clean with a damp paper towel, or rinse well under running water (do not soak in water). Pat them dry with paper towels. Slice off the lower stem end and discard. Slice the rest of the stems and the caps ⅛ to ¼ inch thick. (Mushrooms cook down somewhat so there won't be as much as you might think.)

In a heavy skillet or saucepan, melt the butter over a medium flame until bubbly but not brown. Add the mushrooms and stir to coat them with the butter. Sauté for about 5 minutes, stirring frequently until they brown lightly on all sides.

Toast the bread.

Sprinkle the flour over the mushrooms and stir until the flour has been absorbed. Cook about one minute, stirring, then lower the flame a bit and slowly pour in ¼ cup milk, a little at a time, stirring constantly to form a smooth gravy. Add more milk as desired if the gravy is too thick. Be watchful during the cooking because milk gravy will thicken quickly and also the milk will evaporate by too high cooking heat. Season with salt and pepper, if desired.

Pour a little gravy into a plate or soup plate, add the toast slices, and then pour the remaining mushrooms and gravy over the toast.

Stuffed Mushrooms with Mushroom Filling

With a salad and one or two cooked vegetables, this provides a good quick dinner. Mushrooms are an excellent substitute for meat at a meal. They are also good cold, for lunch. For an elegant and economical hors d'oeuvre to serve to friends, use smaller-sized mushrooms (and increase the number). Make them up ahead of time, and serve at room temperature as "finger food."

6 to 8 2-inch fresh mushrooms, including stems
2 tablespoons butter or margarine, divided
2 to 3 green onions or 1 shallot, finely chopped
½ cup béchamel sauce (recipe follows)
½ teaspoon fresh parsley, finely chopped
Salt and freshly ground white or black pepper to taste
1 tablespoon fine dry bread crumbs
½ teaspoon grated Swiss or Parmesan cheese

Preheat oven to 350° F.

Remove the stems from the mushrooms, and cut off the dried stem ends. Wash the stems and caps, and place them on paper toweling to dry. In a heavy 8-inch to 10-inch skillet, melt 1 tablespoon butter. Add green onions and sauté until soft, stirring so the butter does not burn. Chop the mushroom stems, and, using paper towels, squeeze out as much moisture as you can until the chopped stems are dry. Add them to the onions and cook over moderate heat for about 10 minutes or until all the moisture is gone and the stems and onions are nicely browned. Grease a shallow baking dish, one that is large enough to hold the mushroom caps without crowding. While the stems and onions are cooking, make the béchamel sauce. When the sauce is cooked, remove from the stove and add the onions, mushroom stems, and chopped parsley. Salt the mushroom caps, and spoon the filling into them. Mix the bread crumbs and grated cheese, and sprinkle over the filling. Dot the caps with the remaining 1 tablespoon butter, cut in bits. Bake in the upper third of the oven about 15 minutes, or until the mushrooms are tender when pierced with a fork and the filling is lightly browned. Serve hot or cold.

Béchamel Sauce (White Sauce)
(Makes about ½ cup)

1 tablespoon butter or margarine
1½ tablespoons flour
½ cup hot milk (¼ cup powdered milk and ½ cup water may be substituted)
Salt and pepper, preferably white, to taste

In a heavy 1-quart saucepan, melt the butter and stir in the flour. Cook, stirring constantly, for a couple of minutes, but do not let the mixture brown. Remove the pan from the heat, and gradually blend in the hot milk. Return the pan to a high heat and cook, stirring constantly, until the sauce comes to a boil. Reduce the heat and simmer, stirring rapidly to prevent lumping, for 2 to 3 minutes, or until sauce is thick enough to coat a spoon heavily. Remove from the heat and season with salt and pepper to taste.

Variations: The following additions may be made to the finished sauce. Mix well and return to heat briefly before serving.

• ¼ to ½ cup crab meat, frozen, canned, or fresh (shredded and carefully picked over to remove shell and cartilage bits), and a few drops of lemon juice

• ¼ cup chopped, cooked spinach (squeezed dry) and a bit of finely chopped boiled ham.

• ¼ cup tiny shrimp, chopped, with one small shrimp placed on top of the filling.

Baked Onion

1 large brown Spanish onion
1 tablespoon butter
Seasoned salt and nutmeg to taste

Preheat oven to 350° F.

Peel and core the onion, then make two slashes across the top in a crisscross fashion. Fill the cored hollow of the onion with butter. Sprinkle with seasoned salt and nutmeg. Bake for approximately 1 hour. Serve. (You may also bake in a 400° F. oven for 45 minutes if you wish to prepare it simultaneously with other dishes you are baking.)

Fried Onions

1 to 2 tablespoons butter, margarine, or oil
1 large Spanish onion, sliced thin

Heat the butter or oil in a skillet. When moderately hot, add the sliced onions. Cover the pan (to speed the cooking), and cook about 10 minutes. Uncover the pan and continue cooking until the onions are golden brown and tender. Serve over meat or as a separate vegetable dish.

Creamed Onions

1 to 2 tablespoons butter, margarine, or oil
1 large Spanish onion, sliced thin
2 tablespoons flour (approximately)
¾ cup milk or water (approximately)

In a heavy skillet, heat the butter or oil. When hot, add the onions. Lower heat, and stir so the onions become well coated. Cover and cook until onions are tender, but don't let them brown.

When cooked, sprinkle in the flour and mix well, until all the flour has been moistened with the oil and the onions.

Continue cooking for a minute or so, then slowly pour in the milk or water, stirring constantly. If gravy is too thick, add a bit more liquid until you achieve the consistency you want.

Serve as a separate vegetable or over hamburger patties or steak.

Note: Onions cook down by about one half, so if the pan looks too full when you start, don't worry—it won't be that much when you finish!

Minted Sweet Peas

$\frac{1}{3}$ to $\frac{1}{2}$ cup sweet peas, frozen or fresh
$\frac{1}{2}$ teaspoon granulated sugar
$\frac{1}{8}$ teaspoon crushed mint, fresh or dried
1 tablespoon water
1 tablespoon butter or margarine

Place peas, sugar, mint, and water in a small saucepan with a tight-fitting cover. Cook, uncovered, over high heat until the water begins to simmer. Then, cover and reduce the heat to as low as possible. Cook for 6 to 8 minutes. If steam starts to escape from the pan, slide pan part way off the heat and continue to cook in this fashion. When cooked, drain off any liquid, add the butter, and swirl around until it melts and coats the peas. Serve hot.

Stir-Fried Snow Peas, Mushrooms, and Bamboo Shoots

2 mushrooms, either Chinese dried or fresh, about 1 inch to $1\frac{1}{2}$ inches
  in diameter, quartered
$\frac{1}{4}$ pound fresh or frozen snow peas (Chinese pea pods) If frozen, thaw
  first.
1 scant tablespoon peanut oil or flavorless vegetable oil
$\frac{1}{8}$ cup canned bamboo shoots, sliced $\frac{1}{8}$ inch thick, trimmed into 1 inch
  by 1 inch triangles, or cut in small strips
$\frac{1}{8}$ teaspoon sugar

If you use dried Chinese mushrooms, soak them in a bit of warm water for about 30 minutes. In either case, trim off the mushroom stem ends. Then, from the soaked Chinese mushrooms strain off the water, reserving about 2 teaspoons.

If you use fresh pea pods, snap off the ends and destring.

Heat a skillet at high temperature, and add the oil, then lower to moderate. Drop in the mushrooms and bamboo shoots. Stir-fry for about 2 minutes. Add the pea pods, sugar, and the water reserved from the mushrooms. Cook, stirring constantly, over high heat for a minute or more, until the water evaporates. Remove immediately and serve.

Quick-Fried Peppers and Onions

Vegetable oil, enough to cover vegetables
3 to 4 green onions, including tops, cut in 2-inch pieces
1 green or red bell pepper, cored and seeded and cut into pieces $1\frac{1}{2}$
  inches by 2 inches square

Use a pan large enough so the vegetables won't be crowded. A large skillet or wok is ideal. Heat oil in skillet and when it is hot, carefully slide the cut vegetables into it. Stir around to separate them well. Cook for 2 to 3 minutes, until just barely tender and the skin of the pepper is blistered. Drain on absorbent paper, and serve.

Potatoes Anna

1 medium-sized potato
Bits of butter or margarine
Salt, pepper, and nutmeg to taste

Preheat oven to 400° F.

Heavily grease a small (8-ounce) casserole with a cover (or make a cover using foil). Peel and thinly slice the potato. Line the sides of the casserole with an overlapping layer of potato slices. Place a few slices in the bottom of the casserole, and add bits of butter or margarine, then a little salt, pepper, and nutmeg to taste. Build up layers of potato slices, butter, salt, pepper, and nutmeg alternatingly, until you have used all the slices. Dot the final layer with butter and season it.

Cover the casserole and place it in the oven for about 45 minutes. When the potatoes are fork tender (the way you like to eat them), remove the dish from the oven, run a knife around the inside edge to loosen the potato slices, and invert the dish onto your plate. The potato slices should be nicely browned around the outside and should slip out quite easily, forming a mound on your plate. (If they don't, they will still taste just as good—and will cool more quickly for you!)

Serve with Ground Meat Roll for a nice, easy dinner, with a minimum of clutter and after-dinner dishes. Put the potatoes in the oven first, though—they take a bit longer to bake than the meat does.

French-Fried Potatoes

1 medium potato
Oil for cooking

Peel the potato, and cut into $\frac{1}{4}$-inch slices lengthwise. Next, cut these slices into $\frac{1}{4}$-inch slices. Spread all the slices on a paper towel, and put another layer of toweling on top of them. Pat the potatoes dry.

Place enough oil in a large skillet to fill it $\frac{1}{4}$ inch deep. Skillet should be large enough so potatoes are not crowded. Heat the oil. When it is hot, carefully slide the potato slices into the oil. Cook for 4 to 5 minutes, until soft and golden brown. Remove to paper toweling and sprinkle with salt. Serve hot.

Old-Fashioned Pan-Fried Potatoes

1 medium-sized potato
1 to 2 tablespoons oil for cooking (depending on size of pan)
$\frac{1}{2}$ teaspoon water
Salt and pepper to taste

Peel and cut the potato into round slices, $\frac{1}{8}$ inch to $\frac{1}{4}$ inch thick. (The thinner the slice, the better it will pan-fry.) Heat the oil in a skillet. When it is hot, place the potato slices in the pan, and, using a spatula or pancake turner, turn the potatoes over to coat them with the oil. Add water, and cover the pan, reducing heat. (The water will provide steam and cook the potatoes faster.)

When potatoes are nearly done, remove the cover, raise the heat, and cook, turning once or twice so that potatoes will brown lightly all over. Season with salt and pepper and serve hot.

Variation: Chop 1 medium onion and add to the potatoes at the time you start cooking them. These are called Lyonnaise Potatoes, or, as we called them when we were children, Cowboy Potatoes.

Scalloped Potatoes

1 medium-sized potato, or ½ large potato
1 tablespoon flour
1 tablespoon butter or margarine, cut into bits
½ teaspoon onion powder or ½ small onion, diced
Dash of garlic powder
Salt and pepper to taste
⅓ cup milk

Preheat oven to 400° F.

Peel the potato and slice crosswise, in thin slices. Grease a casserole that is large enough to contain bubbling milk without letting it boil over: about a 1-quart size. Slice the potatoes directly into the casserole or onto a sheet of waxed paper, then put them in the casserole. Sprinkle the flour over the potatoes. Dot them with bits of butter, then sprinkle the onion powder, garlic powder, salt, and pepper over them. Pour in the milk; it should come to about ¾ the depth of the potato slices.

Bake for about 30 minutes. Serve hot.

Potatoes au Gratin

Prepare the same as for Scalloped Potatoes, but add about ¼ cup grated Cheddar cheese. In the casserole, alternate the layers of potatoes and cheese, leaving some cheese to sprinkle over the top of the potatoes. If desired, sprinkle fine bread crumbs over the top layer of cheese. Bake the same as for Scalloped Potatoes.

Oven "Boiled" Potatoes

Though these resemble boiled potatoes, they are baked in the oven and have a slightly different—and interesting—flavor.

1 to 3 potatoes depending on size—new, red, White Rose, or brown potatoes
$\frac{1}{2}$ to 1 tablespoon butter or margarine for each potato
Minced parsley or dill
Salt and pepper to taste

Preheat oven to 400° F.

Wash potatoes, and cut them into bite-sized pieces or small chunks. If you use small new potatoes, there is no need to cut them.

Place the potatoes in a 12-inch square of foil, dot with plenty of butter or margarine, and add a pinch of minced parsley or dill, if you like, along with salt and pepper. Crease the foil edges together tightly and securely so steam won't escape, and put the packet into the oven. Bake for 30 to 45 minutes. Enjoy hot.

Note: You can peel the potatoes before slicing if you must, but remember, the vitamins are in and just beneath the skins. So, if you peel them, you also peel away their good food value. But if you really don't like to eat the skins, peel them off *after* you have cooked the potatoes: at least, that way, the vitamins are cooked back into the potatoes. Besides, as a time- and energy-saver, the skins come off more easily after the potatoes are cooked than when you peel them raw.

Nutmeg Spinach

½ package frozen spinach, chopped
2½ teaspoons butter or margarine
¼ tablespoon flour
2 to 3 teaspoons cream or diluted evaporated milk
Pinch of grated nutmeg

Thaw and drain the spinach. Melt the butter in a saucepan and add the flour, stirring to mix well and break down any lumps. Gradually stir in the cream and continue stirring to a smooth consistency. Cook until thickened, then add the spinach and nutmeg. Cover the pan and cook over a low flame until the spinach is heated through, about 5 minutes. Stir once or twice while the mixture cooks. Serve.

Spinach Chablis

If a whole package of frozen spinach is too much for you to eat at once, use only a half a package.

1 package frozen chopped spinach, cooked and drained
1 tablespoon butter or margarine
1 tablespoon flour
2 tablespoons milk (approximately)
2 tablespoons Chablis or other white wine, or more, to taste
¼ teaspoon nutmeg, or to taste
Pepper to taste

While spinach is cooking, prepare the sauce. Melt the butter in a saucepan and blend in the flour; cook for a minute, stirring constantly. Gradually add the milk, a little at a time, stirring constantly to make a thin, pastelike mixture. Add a little Chablis, stirring constantly, until the sauce is a little thinner. Add a little more milk if sauce is still too thick. Sprinkle in nutmeg and pepper and mix well. Add the drained spinach and stir until the spinach is well coated with the sauce. Serve.

Spinach and Mushrooms

2 to 3 tablespoons butter or margarine, divided
1 packaged frozen chopped spinach
2 to 3 large fresh mushrooms, diced
Salt and pepper to taste
Dash of nutmeg
1 cup grated Swiss or Jack cheese, divided
1 tablespoon fine bread crumbs

Preheat oven to 325° F.

Melt 1 tablespoon butter in saucepan. Add chopped spinach, mushrooms, salt, pepper, and nutmeg. Cover and cook for 2 minutes, until the spinach thaws. Remove cover, raise heat, and stir several times while the moisture evaporates. Add ¼ cup cheese and stir.

Pour mixture into an ungreased casserole, top with the remaining grated cheese, sprinkle the bread crumbs over the top, and dot with bits of remaining butter. Bake for 15 minutes, until the cheese melts.

Delicious with French-fried pounded round steak. Any portion left over can be placed in a covered dish and refrigerated or frozen for later use.

Oven Zucchini

1 to 2 fresh zucchini
Butter or margarine
Salt and pepper to taste

Preheat oven to 375° F.

Wash the zucchini and trim off the ends. Slice the zucchini lengthwise, then, holding the pieces together, give them a half-turn and slice them again lengthwise. This should give you strips about ½ inch square.

Place the zucchini in a small (8-ounce) casserole, a small foil tray, or a large piece of foil. Add the butter, and sprinkle with salt and pepper. Cover the dish (or crimp the edges of the foil together tightly), and place in oven for 20 to 30 minutes. Serve hot.

Variations: Add 1 tomato, chopped, and a sprinkle of basil before baking. Or omit butter and substitute a piece of bacon cut in bits.

14

Pasta, Rice, and One-Dish Meals

Noodles Romanoff

1 rounded cup egg noodles	½ teaspoon onion powder
Water	3 drops Tabasco sauce
2 tablespoons cottage cheese	1 tablespoon chopped green pepper
⅛ teaspoon garlic powder	or pimiento
Dash of Worcestershire sauce	3 teaspoons grated Parmesan
2 tablespoons sour cream	cheese

Preheat oven to 350° F.

In a saucepan, boil the noodles in water until tender, about 10 minutes. Drain. Combine the noodles, cottage cheese, garlic powder, Worcestershire sauce, sour cream, onion powder, Tabasco sauce, and green pepper. Pour into a buttered casserole; sprinkle with Parmesan cheese. Bake uncovered, for 25 minutes, or until heated through.

Baked Macaroni and Cheese

1 cup elbow macaroni
2 quarts water
½ teaspoon vegetable oil

Bring the water to a rolling boil in a 3- to 4-quart saucepan and slowly add macaroni. Stir in oil to keep macaroni from sticking together. Return to the boil and cook over medium heat 10 to 12 minutes, stirring occasionally, until the macaroni is tender but not too soft. When done, pour the macaroni into a colander and let it drain.

Preheat oven to 400° F.

Cheese Sauce

1½ to 2 tablespoons butter or margarine
⅔ cup sharp Cheddar cheese, diced or grated
2 tablespoons flour
½ to ¾ cup milk *or* ⅓ cup powdered milk mixed with ½ to ¾ cup cold water
2 generous dashes of garlic powder
3 dashes of onion powder
1 teaspoon oregano, crushed
Salt and pepper to taste

In a 1-quart saucepan, over moderate heat, melt the butter, and stir in the diced or grated cheese. Stir constantly until the cheese is almost melted. Sprinkle the flour over the mixture and stir continually, moistening all the flour. Continue stirring until the cheese melts, using a wooden spoon to mash the pieces and speed the melting process. Remove the pan from the heat, and stir in a portion of the milk. When it is well mixed with the cheese, pour in a bit more milk and repeat the process until the milk and cheese are blended to a smooth consistency. Return the pan to the heat and stir constantly until the sauce thickens, adding more milk from time to time until all the milk has been added. Add the garlic, onion, and oregano. Bring the mixture to a slight simmer and cook for 2 to 3 minutes, stirring constantly. Add the salt and pepper, and taste for seasoning.

Grease a 2-quart casserole. Pour a bit of the sauce into the bottom of the casserole, add the macaroni, then add the remaining sauce. If desired, sprinkle the top with grated cheese or a cheese-and-bread crumb mixture. Bake 25 to 30 minutes, or until the mixture is "set" but not dry.

Note: While most macaroni-and-cheese recipes call for sharp, medium, or mellow Cheddar cheese, you can inject new taste appeal by using another variety of cheese—for example, a smoked cheese spread, pasteurized processed cheese with caraway seeds, or even fancy cheeses like those one receives on gift cheese trays at Christmas. And you can use either one kind of cheese or several. Try using three or four varieties—the possibilities are intriguing!

The quantity of cheese used in this recipe is based on personal preference. If you like a mild, subtle cheese flavor, use less cheese. If you prefer a strong cheese taste, increase the quantity of cheese. For a crusty, crunchy bottom, sprinkle grated cheese around the dish after you have greased it, then pour in the sauce and macaroni, and bake as directed.

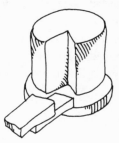

Spaghetti and Quick Tomato Sauce

Sauce

1 8-ounce can tomato sauce
$\frac{1}{2}$ teaspoon olive oil
$\frac{1}{2}$ teaspoon molasses
$\frac{1}{2}$ teaspoon wine vinegar (or plain vinegar)
Pinch each of thyme, rosemary, marjoram, tarragon, oregano (or vary
    quantity to taste)
$\frac{1}{2}$ teaspoon onion powder
$\frac{1}{2}$ teaspoon garlic powder
Dash of celery salt (optional)

Combine all ingredients in a saucepan and stir to blend. Cook over low heat, stirring. Taste for seasoning (flavor will mellow while cooking) and correct if needed. Simmer slowly, uncovered, while the spaghetti water comes to a boil. As sauce thickens, taste again, and adjust the seasoning as needed. Tartness or sweetness is adjusted by adding molasses or vinegar.

For interesting taste variations, add sliced fresh or canned button mushrooms, minced green pepper, or previously browned ground beef or Italian sausage to the tomato sauce.

Spaghetti

2 quarts water
$\frac{1}{4}$ pound spaghetti, or as much as desired
1 tablespoon olive oil
2 dashes garlic powder
Grated Parmesan cheese to taste (optional)

Fill a large kettle with water, leaving sufficient room for spaghetti so it won't boil over onto the stove. Put the water on to boil. Pour in the olive oil, and sprinkle in the garlic powder. When water reaches a fast boil, add spaghetti a handful at a time, pushing it down into the water as it softens. Stir it with a fork to make certain it is not sticking together. Cook at a rapid boil for about 10 minutes, or according to directions on the package. Pour into a colander and drain.

To serve, put the cooked spaghetti on a plate, and spoon the tomato sauce over it. Sprinkle with cheese if you wish.

Italian Meat Sauce

Yield: 2 ½ cups

This sauce is delicious on spaghetti or with lasagna, shell macaroni, or other pasta dishes.

1 pound ground round steak
1 medium onion, chopped fine, *or* 1 tablespoon onion powder
1 clove garlic, minced, *or* ¼ to ½ teaspoon garlic powder
⅛ cup olive oil
1 ½ cans (#303 cans, 8 ounces each) tomatoes
1 can tomato paste
¼ cup water
¼ cup celery, chopped
⅛ cup parsley, chopped
¾ teaspoon salt (optional)
1 teaspoon sugar
⅛ teaspoon pepper
1 bay leaf
½ teaspoon oregano

In a large saucepan, brown the meat, onions, and garlic in oil over moderate heat. Add the remaining ingredients, stirring well, and simmer from 1 to 3 hours, stirring at intervals, until the sauce is thick and smooth. If you prefer a thinner sauce, cook it less than 3 hours (although the longer it cooks, the more robust the flavor).

Sauce will keep well in the refrigerator for several days. It can also be frozen. Allow about 1 cup of sauce for each serving of spaghetti, depending upon how much sauce you like.

Puerto Rican Rice Sanchez

1 teaspoon olive oil (or other vegetable oil)
1/4 cup rice
1/4 cup tomato sauce
1/8 teaspoon onion powder *or* about 1 teaspoon chopped fresh onion
1/8 teaspoon garlic powder *or* about 1 small clove of garlic, minced
1/2 cup water
Salt and pepper to taste (optional)

Heat the oil in a saucepan or skillet (with a tightly fitting cover). When the oil is hot, pour in the rice and stir constantly until it has browned, being careful not to burn the rice. Add the tomato sauce, onion, and garlic, and simmer for a couple of minutes. Add the water and bring to a boil. Boil until about half the water has evaporated, then cover the pan tightly, lower the heat as low as possible, and cook, undisturbed, for about 20 minutes. Salt and pepper may be added if desired. Serve.

Rice Medley

1/4 cup rice
1 teaspoon butter or margarine
1 teaspoon granulated chicken stock base
1/2 cup water
2 slices green pepper, diced
1 2-inch mushroom, diced

In a skillet, cook the rice in the butter, stirring constantly, until rice turns a creamy color. Do not allow the rice to burn.

Add the chicken stock base and water; bring to a boil; cover the pan tightly and lower the flame to the lowest level and cook undisturbed for 10 minutes. Add the green pepper and mushrooms, cover the pan, and continue cooking another 10 minutes, until rice is tender. Fluff with a fork and serve.

Fried Rice with Pork and Vegetables

¼ cup fresh peas, or frozen peas, thawed
1 tablespoon peanut oil or other flavorless vegetable oil, divided
1 egg, lightly beaten
1 cup plain rice, cooked
1 or 2 tablespoons green or red bell pepper, cored, seeded, and diced
¼ cup cooked pork, diced
1 tablespoon minced onion
Salt to taste (optional)

If you are using fresh peas, cook them, uncovered, in boiling water until tender, then drain and run cold water over them to stop the cooking and set the color. Frozen peas need only be thawed.

Assemble all ingredients within easy reach of your stove. Put a few drops of the oil in a heated skillet and swirl it around, then lower the heat to moderate. Pour in the beaten egg. It will form a film on the pan almost at once. Lift this film gently, using a fork or wooden spoon, and push it toward the edge of the pan, allowing the uncooked portion of the egg to spread across the pan to cook. As soon as the egg is set, but before it browns or becomes dry, remove it to a small bowl. Using a fork, break the egg into pieces.

Put the remaining oil in the pan, and heat it for a few seconds, then add the rice and stir-fry for 2 to 3 minutes, until all the grains are coated with the oil. Add the diced peppers, peas, and pork, and stir-fry for about 1 minute more. Put the egg back into the pan, and add the minced onion. Stir-fry only long enough to reheat the egg. Season with salt if desired. Serve at once.

Fried Rice with Ham and Egg

$\frac{1}{4}$ cup frozen peas, thawed, or fresh peas, shelled
1 tablespoon peanut oil or other flavorless vegetable oil, divided
1 egg, lightly beaten
1 cup plain rice, cooked
$\frac{1}{2}$ teaspoon salt
$\frac{1}{4}$ cup cooked ham, diced
1 small green onion, including top, finely chopped

If you are using fresh peas, cook them, uncovered, in boiling water for a few minutes, until tender, then drain them and run cold water over them to stop the cooking and set the color. Frozen peas need only to be thawed.

Place a few drops of the oil in a heated skillet and swirl it around the pan, then immediately lower the heat to moderate. Pour in the beaten egg. It will form a film on the bottom of the pan almost at once. Lift this film gently, using a fork, and push it toward the edge of the pan, allowing the uncooked portion of the egg to spread across the pan to cook. As soon as the egg is set, but before it browns or becomes dry, remove it to a small bowl, and break up the cooked egg with a fork.

Put the remaining oil into the pan, and heat it for a few seconds. Then, add the rice and stir-fry 2 to 3 minutes, until all the grains are coated with oil. Add the salt, peas, and ham, and stir-fry for about $\frac{1}{2}$ minute more. Put the egg back into the pan and add the green onion. Stir-fry only long enough to reheat the egg. Serve at once. This is a nice substitute for plain boiled rice with almost any dinner.

Quick Baked Beans

1 13-ounce can baked beans
$\frac{1}{4}$ cup molasses
3 teaspoons brown sugar
$\frac{1}{8}$ teaspoon powdered ginger
$\frac{1}{8}$ teaspoon dry mustard
1 generous dash garlic powder

2 generous dashes powdered onion *or* 1 tablespoon raw onion, minced
1 drop Liquid Smoke

Preheat oven to 400° F.

Mix all the ingredients together in a small ovenproof casserole. Cover and bake for about 30 minutes, or until most of the liquid has cooked away. Serve hot.

Variation: Add 1 to 2 slices chopped bacon, cooked or raw, before baking.

Tomato-Cheese Pie

1 unbaked pie shell
Olive oil
1 medium tomato
2 to 3 green onions
1 small to medium green bell pepper, cored and seeded
Pinch of oregano *or* sweet basil
3 to 4 slices Gruyère or Swiss cheese *or* ¼ to ½ cup grated
Black pepper (optional)

Preheat oven to 400° F.

Brush the unbaked pie shell generously with olive oil. Slice the tomato, and arrange the slices on the pie shell, overlapping them if necessary. Dice the green onions, along with about 2 inches of their tops, and sprinkle them over the tomatoes. Dice the green pepper and sprinkle it over the tomatoes as evenly as possible. Crush a pinch of oregano or sweet basil between your fingers and sprinkle it over all. Cut the cheese into strips, about 5 strips per slice, and lay the slices closely together over the top so that the entire top is covered with the cheese. Dribble olive oil over the cheese, and, if desired, grind black pepper over it. Bake approximately 20 minutes, till cheese is melted.

This is also good chilled or at room temperature, which means it is good as a take-along lunch for working days.

Variation: For interesting variety, sliced fresh mushrooms may be added to the vegetables, as well as parboiled eggplant cut into slices or cubes.

Cheese Soufflé

2 to 2½ tablespoons butter or margarine, divided
½ cup (or more to taste) grated imported Swiss cheese *or* ¼ cup each
   Swiss and freshly grated Parmesan cheese
1½ tablespoons flour
½ cup hot milk
¼ teaspoon salt
Pinch of white pepper
2 egg yolks
3 egg whites

Preheat oven to 400° F.

    Butter the bottom and side of a 1- to 2-quart French soufflé dish or glass casserole with ½ to 1 tablespoon butter, then sprinkle it with ½ to 1 tablespoon grated Swiss cheese, tipping the dish to spread the cheese as evenly as possible on the bottom and all sides. Set aside.

    In a 2-quart saucepan, melt the remaining 1½ tablespoons butter over moderate heat. When the foam subsides, stir in the flour, using a wooden spoon. Cook over low heat, stirring constantly, for 1 to 2 minutes, being careful not to let the mixture brown. Remove from heat and pour in the hot milk, a little at a time, beating until the mixture is well blended. Add the salt and pepper. Return to low heat and cook, stirring constantly, until the sauce comes to a boil and is smooth and thick. Simmer a moment, then remove from heat and beat in the egg yolks, one at a time, until each one is thoroughly blended. Set aside.

    Using a whisk, or a rotary or electric beater, beat the egg whites until they are stiff and form small points that stand straight up. (It is best to use a copper bowl for this, if you have one.) Stir a big spoonful of beaten egg white into the sauce, then stir in all but 1 tablespoon of the remaining grated cheese. With a spatula, lightly fold in the rest of the egg whites, using a cutting rather than a stirring motion.

    Gently pour the soufflé mixture into the prepared dish; it should be about ¾ full. Lightly smooth the surface with a spatula, and sprinkle the remaining cheese over the top. For a decorative effect, make a "cap" on the soufflé with a spatula by cutting a trench about 1 inch deep and 1 inch from the rim all around the dish.

    Place the soufflé on the middle shelf of the oven, and immediately lower the heat to 375° F. Bake 25 to 30 minutes, or until the soufflé puffs up about 2 inches above the rim of the dish and the top grows lightly browned. Serve at once.

Serving suggestion: To make this soufflé a more hearty dish, add 2 or 3 shelled, whole hard-cooked eggs, or, if preferred, cut them into quarters or eighths. You may also add any of a variety of quick-cooking vegetables, bits of meat, and so on. To do this, pour about half the soufflé mixture into the soufflé dish, arrange the eggs, vegetables, and/or meat on top, and then pour in the remaining soufflé mixture.

Vegetable Pie

This is reminiscent of a pizza, but does not contain meat or sauce. It makes a delicious one-dish dinner and is also good cold, for instance, as a take-along lunch for work.

1 baked and cooled 9-inch pie shell, homemade or purchased
¼ pound Swiss cheese, sliced thin, or substitute any cheese desired
1 or 2 fresh tomatoes, medium size, sliced
1 or 2 sprigs of fresh parsley, chopped fine
1 zucchini, cut into ¼-inch slices
2 green onions, including the tops, sliced
1 2-inch mushroom, diced
½ green pepper, cored, seeded, and cut into small pieces
2 tablespoons grated Parmesan cheese
1 teaspoon oregano *or* sweet basil
Ground black pepper to taste
2 tablespoons olive oil

Preheat oven to 375° F.

Cover the bottom of the pie crust with overlapping slices of cheese. Add the tomato slices, then layer on the parsley, zucchini, green onions, mushroom, and green pepper. Sprinkle the Parmesan cheese, oregano or basil, and black pepper over the top. Dribble the olive oil over all. Bake about 25 minutes.

Variation: To use as finger food for a cocktail party, cut the pie into small pieces about 1 inch by 2 inches. Add anchovies or sardines, cut in small pieces, or smoked oysters, if desired.

Eggplant Parmigiana

$\frac{1}{2}$ medium- to large-sized eggplant
Salt
1 large or 2 small fresh tomatoes, peeled and diced
2 rounded teaspoons tomato paste
$2\frac{1}{2}$ tablespoons olive oil, divided
$\frac{1}{4}$ cup fine bread crumbs
1 tablespoon grated Parmesan cheese
1 or 2 sprigs fresh parsley, chopped
Generous dash of garlic powder
Pepper, to taste
3 or 4 thin slices mozzarella cheese

Preheat oven to 375° F.

Wash the eggplant and slice into $\frac{1}{2}$-inch-thick slices; there should be about 3 slices. (You may peel eggplant if you wish, but it isn't necessary if the fruit is young.) Sprinkle the slices with salt and allow to stand for a few minutes on paper towels to draw out the excess moisture.

Cook the tomato, tomato paste, and 2 teaspoons olive oil in a 1-quart saucepan for about 15 minutes, over low heat. Stir a few times to prevent burning or sticking to the pan. The mixture will become fairly thick.

Heat the remaining oil in a heavy skillet and when hot, sauté the eggplant slices over medium heat until they are soft and lightly browned. Drain the pieces on paper toweling.

Grease a baking dish about 2 inches deep and large enough to hold the largest slice of eggplant; a foil pan 3 inches by 5 inches by $2\frac{1}{2}$ inches is perfect. Make alternate layers of eggplant and the sauce and crumbs as follows: 1 teaspoon or so of sauce on bottom of casserole; 1 slice of eggplant, $\frac{1}{3}$ sauce, $\frac{1}{3}$ bread crumb mixture. Repeat until the eggplant slices are used. Place thinly sliced mozzarella cheese over the top. Bake until the cheese is slightly browned and bubbly, about 10 minutes. Serve.

Hurry-Up Eggplant Parmigiana

2 or 3 slices eggplant, ½-inch thick
Salt
1 6-ounce can tomato paste
2½ tablespoons olive oil, divided
2 dashes garlic powder
Dash of onion powder
¼ cup bread crumbs, fine
1 or 2 sprigs of fresh parsley
3 or 4 slices mozzarella cheese, sliced thin

Preheat oven to 375° F.
Sprinkle eggplant with salt and let stand on paper towels a few minutes to drain out extra moisture. Cut the slices into cubes. Simmer the tomato paste, 2 teaspoons olive oil, dashes of garlic powder and onion powder until hot and oil is well blended into mixture.

Mix the bread crumbs, parsley, garlic powder.

Heat the remaining olive oil in a skillet and add the eggplant cubes. Sauté quickly until browned on all sides. Drain on paper toweling, then put cubes into a greased baking dish. Pour in the tomato paste mixture and the bread crumb mixture. Mix all together in the dish. Top with slices of mozzarella cheese and brown in the oven until the cheese is bubbly.

Chilis Rellenos

2 whole canned chili peppers or whole small parboiled green bell peppers
2 large slices mozzarella cheese, $\frac{1}{8}$ inch thick, cut from a 1-pound ball
1 tablespoon plus 1 teaspoon flour, divided
1 egg, separated
Olive oil for sautéing

Core the peppers and remove the seeds; leave peppers whole. Cut each slice of mozzarella cheese into 3 long strips. Place these strips into each pepper, gently pushing them in to fill the cavity. Roll the stuffed peppers in the tablespoon of flour spread onto a sheet of wax paper, coating all sides well, patting in the flour in spots if needed.

Beat the egg white in a wide shallow dish until it holds a stiff peak. Sprinkle in 1 teaspoon of flour and fold the flour into the egg white. Beat the egg yolk separately and fold it into the whites.

Heat the oil to 275° F. in an electric frying pan, or over moderate flame on stove, using a heavy skillet. While the oil heats, roll the floured peppers in the egg mixture, coating the peppers heavily. Sauté to a golden brown on each side, turning once. Remove to absorbent paper to drain. Serve with Puerto Rican Rice Sanchez (page 156) and Rellenos Sauce (recipe follows), spooning sauce over the Rellenos.

Chili Rellenos Sauce

1 teaspoon olive oil
$\frac{1}{4}$ cup tomato sauce
Dash of onion powder
Dash of garlic powder
Pinch of oregano

Simmer all ingredients together in a small saucepan over moderate heat. Do not let sauce burn. Cook just long enough to heat and blend the flavors.

Stuffed Bell Pepper

1 large green bell pepper, cored and seeded
$\frac{1}{4}$ pound lean ground beef
$\frac{1}{8}$ cup rice, cooked
Dash of garlic powder
Dash of onion powder
Dash of Kitchen Bouquet or other meat flavoring
Dash of freshly ground pepper
1 recipe of Tomato Sauce (recipe follows)

Preheat oven to 350° F.

Place the pepper in a small baking dish or casserole with a cover. Mix the meat, rice, and seasonings, and spoon into the pepper. Pour tomato sauce over the pepper and bake for approximately 45 minutes, covered.

Tomato Sauce

1 8-ounce can tomato sauce
Dash of garlic powder
Dash of onion powder
Pinch of celery seed (optional)
Pinch of tarragon
$\frac{1}{4}$ to $\frac{1}{2}$ teaspoon molasses

Combine all ingredients and simmer in a saucepan over moderate heat to blend the flavors, then pour over the stuffed pepper and bake.

To cook the rice: If you have no leftover rice to use, mix $\frac{1}{8}$ cup rice (2 tablespoons) with $\frac{1}{4}$ cup (4 tablespoons) cold water in a saucepan. Bring to a boil, cover, and cook over very low heat for about 20 minutes, or until water is absorbed. Remove from heat and fluff.

This Stuffed Bell Pepper dish can be frozen before or after it is baked. You may want to make a *double* recipe and store the extra serving in the freezer for another night. To cook or heat frozen Stuffed Bell Pepper, place it in a 350° F. to 400° F. oven, and cook for about 45 minutes. If it is frozen, it may require a few additional minutes to thaw before it actually begins to cook.

Mexican Beef Casserole

$\frac{1}{4}$ to $\frac{1}{3}$ cup uncooked rice
1 tablespoon flour
Chili powder, garlic powder, onion powder, salt, and pepper to taste
$\frac{1}{4}$ to $\frac{1}{2}$ pound ground beef
1 medium-sized can tomatoes (16 ounces)
1 small can whole kernel corn (8 ounces) *or* $\frac{1}{2}$ cup frozen corn

Preheat oven to 375° F.

Place the rice on the bottom of a casserole. Sprinkle a bit of the flour, chili powder, garlic powder, onion powder, salt, and pepper over it. Add a layer of meat, patting it out to a uniform size, and sprinkle again with flour and seasonings. Pour in the canned tomatoes, and add another sprinkling of flour and seasonings, then top with the corn.

Cover the casserole and bake in a moderate oven (350° to 400°) for about 30 minutes, until the rice and meat are cooked. Since the liquid in the tomatoes may vary, check the casserole once or twice during baking; you may have to add a bit more liquid if the juice is absorbed before the rice is fully cooked.

Variation: Substitute ground lean pork or veal for the beef.

Sanchez Sandwich (Grilled Cheese Sandwich)

2 slices white bread
Butter or margarine to taste
Mayonnaise to taste
$\frac{1}{4}$ to $\frac{1}{2}$ cup grated yellow cheese (Cheddar, longhorn, etc.)
Onion powder to taste
Garlic powder to taste
Taco sauce, red or green, to taste

Set a heavy skillet on stove and let it heat while you prepare the sandwich.

Butter the bread, then spread with mayonnaise. Using a hand-held grater, grate enough cheese onto one slice of bread to cover the bread thoroughly, about $\frac{1}{4}$ to $\frac{1}{2}$ inch thick. Sprinkle with onion and garlic powder. Sprinkle a few drops of the taco sauce over the filling; the amount depends on your taste for taco sauce. Do not put all the sauce in one place, but distribute the drops over the surface of the filling.

Put the two slices of bread together, as for a regular sandwich. Spread the top surface with butter. Place in the skillet with the buttered side down. While the sandwich is browning on the bottom side, spread the butter on the now-exposed top surface. When first side is nicely browned, turn the sandwich over, using a wide spatula, and brown the second side. Remove to a piece of absorbent paper and cut the sandwich in half or into quarters. Serve hot. Excellent served with a glass of cold milk.

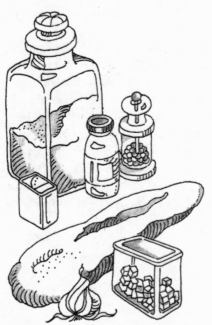

15

Sauces, Relishes, and Garnishes

Basic White Sauce

Yield: ½ cup

	Thin	*Medium*	*Thick*
	(For creamed vegetables, soup base)	*(For creamed and scalloped dishes)*	*(For croquettes, soufflés)*
Butter or margarine	1½ teaspoons	1 tablespoon	2 tablespoons
Flour	1½ to 3 teaspoons	1 tablespoon	2 tablespoons
Salt	to taste	to taste	to taste
Pepper	to taste	to taste	to taste
Milk*	½ cup	½ cup	½ cup

*For a richer sauce, use cream.

Melt butter in a heavy saucepan over low heat. Blend in flour and seasonings. Cook over low heat about 1 minute, stirring until mixture is smooth and bubbly.

Remove pan from heat. Add milk, a little at a time, stirring continuously, until sauce is smooth. A whisk is useful for this purpose. Return pan to heat and bring mixture to a boil, stirring constantly. Cook 1 minute or until the proper consistency.

Variations (Use Medium White Sauce recipe):

Cheese Sauce: Add $\frac{1}{4}$ teaspoon dry mustard with the seasonings. After the milk is added, blend in $\frac{1}{4}$ cup grated sharp or medium Cheddar cheese. Stir until cheese is melted. Use on vegetables, rice, macaroni, and egg dishes.

Mushroom Sauce: Sauté $\frac{1}{2}$ cup sliced mushrooms and $\frac{1}{2}$ teaspoon grated onion or $\frac{1}{4}$ teaspoon onion powder in the butter before adding the flour.

Seafood Sauce: Carefully stir into finished sauce $\frac{1}{4}$ to $\frac{1}{2}$ cup tuna, cooked shrimp, crab meat, lobster, or cooked fish, broken into tiny pieces.

Curry Sauce: Sauté $\frac{1}{4}$ to $\frac{1}{2}$ teaspoon curry powder in the butter before adding the flour and other seasonings. Use on chicken, lamb, shrimp, and rice.

Egg Sauce: Gently stir into the finished sauce 1 diced hard-cooked egg. Season. Especially nice over spinach.

Lemon Sauce for Vegetables

1 egg
$\frac{1}{2}$ tablespoon water
1 tablespoon lemon juice
$\frac{1}{2}$ tablespoon beef or chicken stock

In a heavy saucepan, beat the egg and water until fluffy. Add the lemon juice and stock. Cook over low flame, stirring constantly and quickly to prevent burning and to keep egg from setting too quickly. As soon as sauce thickens, remove from heat and let stand for about 5 minutes. Serve over green vegetables, such as spinach, beans, broccoli, or Brussels sprouts.

Pineapple Sweet-Sour Sauce

This is good as a vegetable dish by itself, with rice, or as a garnish for fish, chicken, or pork.

1 or 2 boiling onions, quartered
2 or 3 slices green pepper, diced
½ cup crushed pineapple, undrained
3 teaspoons vinegar
2 teaspoons brown sugar
¼ cup water or chicken broth
1 teaspoon cornstarch dissolved in 2 teaspoons water

In a skillet or saucepan, simmer the onion, green pepper, pineapple, vinegar, and brown sugar in water or broth until the vegetables are barely tender but still crisp, 5 to 10 minutes. Add the water mixed with the cornstarch and cook, stirring, until thickened. Serve.

Quick Vegetable Topping

1 or 2 tablespoons mayonnaise
Dash of soy sauce
Few drops lemon juice

Combine all ingredients in a small dish, taste for seasonings and correct if necessary. Serve over hot cooked broccoli, zucchini, asparagus, cauliflower, or other vegetables.

You can make this in a larger quantity and keep in the refrigerator in a sealed container.

Sautéed Parsley Relish
(To serve with steaks)

2 teaspoons olive oil for sautéing
1 cup fresh parsley, coarsely chopped
½ teaspoon garlic powder
1 teaspoon Italian herbs
¼ teaspoon celery seed
½ teaspoon Lemon Pepper
2 shallots or green onions, thinly sliced

Heat the oil in a skillet. Add the parsley, garlic, herbs, celery seed, Lemon Pepper, and shallots, and stir until all are lightly oiled. Sauté until shallots and parsley are tender and well browned, about 5 minutes. Stir occasionally to prevent sticking and burning. When done, the relish will be dark in color and quite zesty.

Seasoned Flour

1 cup white flour
Generous dashes of salt, pepper, garlic powder, onion powder, seasoned salt (optional), and paprika

Pour the flour into a plastic bag. Add the other seasonings, using more of the ones you like better. Be especially generous with the paprika. Shake bag to mix all ingredients. The resulting mixture should smell quite spicy, but blended.

Use for coating round steak, chicken, chicken livers, and cubed meat (as in Stroganoff), as well as for flouring fish and seafood.

After using, sift remaining mixture to remove any meat, chicken, or fish particles that may have fallen into it. Return the sifted flour to a plastic bag, and store in the refrigerator up to 1 week.

Garlic Croutons

White bread, sourdough French bread, or leftover French rolls (amount
as desired)
1 tablespoon olive oil
1 garlic clove, crushed, *or* ¼ teaspoon garlic powder

Cut bread into cubes about ½ inch square.

In a heavy skillet, combine oil with garlic, and heat. When the oil
is hot, but not smoking, add the bread cubes. Toss until they are gold-
en brown on all sides. Do not let them burn. Remove and drain on absorbent paper (paper towels or a piece of brown paper bag).

Use in soups or salads.

Variations: Instead of garlic, you might like to try onion powder, or a
combination of garlic powder and onion powder. For herbed croutons,
substitute Italian herbs for the garlic. There are numerous other varieties of croutons you can make just by experimenting with the ingredients on your spice rack.

Croutons will keep nicely for a short time in your refrigerator or
on the pantry shelf if you store them in an airtight container.

Bread Crumbs

Preheat oven to 275° F.
Use fresh bread or rolls, or dry, leftover bread slices. Place the bread,
sliced, on a cookie sheet and dry in the oven at 250° to 300° F. until
crisp but not browned. Remove from the oven.

Break the bread slices into pieces. Then, put the pieces, a few at a
time, into the blender. Set the blender to the "fine" grind, and turn it
on, grinding the pieces into crumbs. (If you don't have a blender, put
the pieces of bread on a sheet of wax paper, and go over them with a
rolling pin or bottle until they are broken down into fine bread
crumbs.)

Store in an airtight jar in the cupboard, refrigerator, or freezer.

You can use any type of bread to make crumbs, but keep rye bread
crumbs separate from white or wheat bread crumbs.

16

Breads and Desserts

White Bread

This recipe makes 1 loaf of bread. You can also divide the dough and use one half to make a small loaf of bread and the other half for rolls.

1 package dry yeast
$\frac{1}{4}$ cup warm water
2 to 4 tablespoons plus 1 teaspoon sugar
1 cup warm milk or water
1 tablespoon oil, melted butter or margarine
1 to $1\frac{1}{2}$ teaspoons salt
3 cups flour, divided

Mix yeast, water, and 1 teaspoon sugar in small bowl. Let stand for 10 to 15 minutes until yeast mixture bubbles and is doubled in size.

In a large bowl mix milk, oil, 2 to 4 tablespoons sugar, salt, and 1 to 1½ cups flour, then add yeast mixture. Beat well to a consistency of thick pancake batter. Let stand in a warm, draft-free place (such as an unlighted oven) for 20 to 30 minutes, until mixture becomes spongy.

When spongy, add another 1½ cups (or more) flour, mixing until dough pulls away from sides of bowl and can be formed into a ball. Turn out onto floured breadboard and knead until elastic, adding more flour to the board if necessary to keep hands from sticking to the dough. Knead about 10 minutes.

Grease the mixing bowl and return the dough to the bowl, turning dough over and over to coat it. Cover the bowl with a towel and set the bowl in an unlighted oven or other draft-free, warm place. Let rise until double in bulk, about 1 hour.

When dough has doubled, punch down and knead again for a few minutes. Then return to bowl, cover with towel, and set in a warm place until doubled again, about 1 hour.

Grease a bread pan. When dough has doubled, punch down again and shape into loaf in pan. Cover with the towel and allow the dough to double again in a warm place. If you are using the oven for this, remove the pan when the dough has doubled, and preheat oven to 350° F. Bake bread for about 40 minutes. Bread will sound hollow when thumped with your knuckles and will be golden brown when baked. Remove from oven and slide loaf out of pan. Grease the top of the loaf with melted butter, or brush with milk for a soft crust. For a crunchier crust, pat sparingly with water. When cool, slice and serve.

If baking a small loaf and rolls, reduce baking time to about 20 to 25 minutes. Use thump method and color to test for doneness.

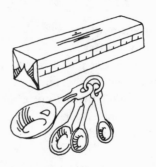

Bea's Bran Muffins

Yield: 30 muffins

The batter for these muffins keeps well in the refrigerator for several weeks, so that you can bake them when you feel like it—one muffin at a time or the entire batch. Once baked, they keep well for about 3 days, or indefinitely if placed in plastic bags and frozen. They thaw quickly.

1 cup Nabisco bran flakes
2 cups Kellogg's All-Bran cereal
1 cup boiling water
1 cup white sugar
½ cup molasses
1 cup oil
2 eggs
2 cups buttermilk
2⅓ cups regular flour
½ teaspoon salt
2½ teaspoons baking soda

Preheat oven to 400° F.

Place the bran flakes and All-Bran in a bowl, and add the boiling water. Mix well to moisten, then set aside. In another bowl, blend together the sugar, molasses, oil, eggs, buttermilk, flour, salt, and baking soda, mixing well. Add the bran mixture to the batter and stir until it is well distributed and blended, and lump-free. Grease the muffin tin. (If you use muffin liners, they do not require greasing.) Fill each about two-thirds full. You may bake a half-dozen, or you may bake the entire recipe. Bake for 15 minutes. Cover any remaining batter tightly and store in the refrigerator for future use.

Variations: Instead of the ½ cup molasses and 1 cup sugar, substitute 1½ cups sugar, or 1 cup sugar with ½ cup honey, or 1¼ cups sugar with ¼ cup molasses. Add 1 cup of raisins, nuts, or dates to the batter.

Note: Should you store unused batter in the refrigerator, mix it well when you remove it. When baking with chilled batter, add 5 minutes to baking time. To reduce the amount of baking time, leave the filled muffin tins on the drainboard until the batter reaches room temperature. Then bake for just 15 minutes.

Cinnamon Rolls

These take longer to describe than they do to make. If you wish to have these rolls for breakfast, prepare them the day before. They are not difficult to make, but since there are several waiting periods between the steps, they are good to prepare on a day you'll be at home.

1 package dry yeast
3 to 4 tablespoons sugar, divided
$\frac{1}{4}$ cup warm water
1 egg
$\frac{1}{2}$ cup warm milk or water
2 tablespoons oil or melted butter or margarine
1 teaspoon cardamom (optional)
$\frac{1}{2}$ to $\frac{3}{4}$ teaspoon salt
2 to 3 cups flour

Add the yeast and 1 teaspoon sugar to the water in a small bowl; stir until dissolved. Set in a warm, draft-free place (85° F.), such as an unlighted oven, until yeast starts to foam—about 5 to 10 minutes. Mix egg, milk, oil, cardamom, salt, and 3 tablespoons sugar. Add yeast mixture and stir to blend. Add 1 to 1$\frac{1}{2}$ cups flour, or enough to produce a consistency of thick pancake batter. Beat well. Cover bowl with a towel. Let stand again in warm place for about 30 minutes, until batter becomes spongy.

When spongy, remove from oven and add another 1 to 1$\frac{1}{2}$ cups flour, mixing until dough pulls away from the bowl. Turn out onto a lightly floured breadboard or kitchen table, and knead until the dough becomes elastic to touch; when spread out or pulled it should spring right back to shape. This takes about 10 minutes. Add more flour, sparingly, as you need it to keep hands from sticking to the dough.

Grease the mixing bowl and return the kneaded dough to the bowl, turning the dough over and over to coat it. Cover the bowl with a towel and set in a warm place, until the dough doubles in bulk. This will take about 1 hour or so.

When doubled, punch dough down and knead again for a few moments. Again, cover the bowl with the towel and let set in a warm place until doubled again in bulk.

To Form Rolls

½ cup butter, softened, divided
1 cup brown sugar, divided
¼ cup cinnamon (approximately), divided

Dust breadboard with flour, sparingly, but enough so that dough does not stick to board. Turn dough out onto board and roll with a rolling pin or a smooth-sided bottle (such as a wine bottle) until about ¼ inch thick. Spread with ½ cup softened butter. Sprinkle ½ cup of brown sugar over the butter, patting it down and distributing it evenly over dough. Over this sprinkle 1 to 2 tablespoons cinnamon, according to taste.

Starting at wide side of dough, roll it into a cylinder, patting the edges to help it stay in position. Using a very sharp knife, cut the cylinder into slices about 1 inch thick.

Into a pan about 9 inches by 9 inches by 2 inches put about ¼ cup butter, about ½ cup brown sugar and 2 tablespoons cinnamon. Melt the butter over a low flame, stirring constantly until sugar melts. Smooth mixture over pan so it is evenly distributed. Place rolls, cut side down, into mixture; leave about ¾ to 1 inch between each roll to allow for rising. Syrup should come partway up the rolls. If there is enough syrup in the pan, spoon some over the tops of the rolls.

Cover the rolls with the towel and return to the unlighted oven, or other draft-free, warm area, to rise again, until double in bulk.

When rolls have doubled, set aside. Light the oven, allowing it to preheat to 350° F. Bake the rolls 20 to 30 minutes, or until the tops are browned and rolls are cooked through. Remove from oven; place a plate upside down over the top of the pan and invert the pan of rolls onto the plate. Cool before serving.

Peach-Pecan Rolls

The Yeast Mixture

2 tablespoons lukewarm water (110° to 115° F.)
½ package (1⅛ teaspoons) active dry yeast
½ teaspoon sugar

Put the water in a small, deep dish. Sprinkle in the yeast, then the sugar; mix to blend. Let mixture stand for about 5 minutes, then stir gently with a fork. Place in a warm, draft-free area until it doubles in bulk, about 10 to 15 minutes. An unlighted oven is ideal for this.

The Dough Mixture

1½ cups unsifted flour
¼ cup sugar
1 teaspoon ground cardamom
½ cup lukewarm milk (110° to 115° F.)
1 egg yolk

In a large mixing bowl, place the flour, sugar, and cardamom, and mix thoroughly. Make a well in the flour. Add the yeast mixture, the milk, and the egg yolk. Stir slowly until the flour is moistened, then stir dough until it is smooth and can be gathered into a ball. Turn the dough out onto a floured surface—cutting board or tabletop—and knead for 10 minutes, until firm. You may add up to ¼ cup more flour, 1 tablespoon at a time, to the board, as needed. Knead until the dough is smooth, elastic, and shiny. Coat the mixing bowl with butter or oil, then return the dough to the bowl, rolling it around until the dough is lightly oiled. Cover the bowl with a dry tea towel and place in an unlighted oven or other warm, draft-free place. Let rise until it is double in bulk. This will take about 1 hour.

The Topping

½ cup peach preserves (or jam)
½ teaspoon cornstarch
½ cup finely chopped pecans
1 teaspoon ground nutmeg
1 tablespoon butter or margarine, chilled and diced

Mix all ingredients except butter in a small bowl. Spread the mixture evenly over the bottom of a 9-inch round baking pan. Sprinkle the butter bits over the top of the mixture, and set the pan aside.

The Filling

¼ cup peach preserves (or jam)
1 teaspoon ground nutmeg
¼ teaspoon cornstarch
1½ tablespoons melted butter or margarine

Mix all the ingredients, except melted butter, in a sauce dish. Set aside.

When the dough has doubled in bulk, remove the tea towel. With one fast blow to the center of the dough, punch the dough down, and turn out onto a lightly floured board. Roll the dough into a rectangle about 9 inches by 5 inches and about ¼ inch thick. Brush the dough with the melted butter, and sprinkle the nutmeg-preserve filling over that, keeping it as uniform as possible. Gently press the filling into the dough.

Starting at the long side of the dough, roll it into a cylinder. Using a very sharp knife, cut the dough into 7 or 8 slices about 1¼ inches thick. Place these pieces, cut side up, into a baking pan, leaving as much space as possible between each roll. Again, cover with the tea towel and let rise until double in bulk. This will take about 45 minutes.

Preheat the oven to 350° F. (If you are using the oven to raise the rolls, remove rolls to the top of the stove or some other warm, draft-free place while the oven preheats.)

When the rolls are doubled in bulk and the oven is hot, brush melted butter over the tops of the rolls. Place in the oven center and bake for 20 to 25 minutes, until rolls are nicely browned. Cool for 5 minutes, then invert the pan onto a wire rack. Cool to at least lukewarm before eating.

Chocolate Éclairs

½ cup water
2 tablespoons plus ½ teaspoon butter or margarine
½ cup regular flour, sifted before measuring
Dash of salt
1 egg
¼ cup Cream Filling (see below)
¼ cup chocolate bits
Few drops milk

Preheat oven to 425° F.

In a saucepan, bring water and 2 tablespoons butter to the boiling point, then add flour and salt quickly. Cook and stir until it is well blended and the dough leaves the sides of the pan and can be formed into a ball. Remove from the fire and add the egg, beating extremely well to blend the egg into the mixture.

Grease a cookie sheet or shallow pie tin. Divide the dough in half and drop both halves onto cookie sheet. Shape the batter with a spoon into oblongs, heaping the dough well along the center. Place the 2 éclairs 2 inches apart on the baking sheet. Bake at 425° F. for 20 minutes, then reduce heat to 350° and bake for another 20 minutes, until éclairs are golden brown without burning the bottom.

Remove from the oven and allow to cool on a wire rack. When cool, use a table fork to pierce the circumference near the top and remove tops. Leave the largest part of the éclair on the bottom. If some of the dough has not completely puffed, remove it from the shell. Do not throw it away—mix it with any leftover filling and eat it; not pretty, but tasty.

Fill the éclairs with Cream Filling, or any other filling you desire. Replace the tops and ice with the following: In a small saucepan, melt the chocolate bits and ½ teaspoon butter, stirring constantly. Add a few drops of milk if mixture is too stiff to spread easily. When blended, gently spread on tops of éclairs.

Cream Filling

¼ cup plus 2 tablespoons sugar (or 6 tablespoons)
1 tablespoon butter or margarine
8 teaspoons flour (or 2 tablespoons plus 2 teaspoons)
1 egg, well beaten
1 cup milk
¼ teaspoon vanilla extract

Combine the sugar, butter, flour, and egg in a saucepan, mixing very well. Slowly add the milk, stirring constantly. Cook over low flame, still stirring constantly, until the filling is thick and smooth. Remove from heat and add the vanilla extract, stirring until it is blended into mixture.

Alternate cooking method: Instead of cooking over a direct flame, use a double boiler. After the milk has been blended into the dry ingredients, cook over boiling water. This eliminates the constant stirring and also the possibility of scorching, but it takes a little longer.

Use to fill cream puffs, éclairs, small individual pie shells, or use as a pudding.

Variations: For pie or pudding, the flavor can be changed by adding different extracts, such as a bit of lemon or orange, or banana flavoring. In pie or pudding, sliced bananas may be added.

Cream Puffs

Delicious and very easy to make.

$\frac{1}{2}$ cup water
2 tablespoons butter or margarine
$\frac{1}{2}$ cup regular flour, sifted before measuring
Dash of salt
1 egg
$\frac{1}{4}$ cup whipped cream sweetened with 1 teaspoon sugar and a few
    drops vanilla extract *or* Cream Filling (see below)
$\frac{1}{4}$ teaspoon confectioners' sugar, sifted, for dusting baked tops

Preheat oven to 425° F.

In a saucepan, bring water and butter to the boiling point, then add the flour and salt quickly. Cook and stir until it is well blended and the dough leaves the sides of the pan and can be formed into a ball. Remove from the fire and add the egg, beating extremely well to blend the egg into the mixture.

Grease a cookie sheet or shallow pie tin. Divide the dough in half, and drop both halves onto cookie sheet. Gently shape the sides of each piece of dough so it is round; the top may or may not be rounded, as you desire. Place the 2 puffs 2 inches apart on the baking sheet. Bake at 425° F. for 20 minutes, then reduce heat to 350° and bake for another 20 minutes, until puffs are a golden brown without burning the bottom.

Remove the puffs from the oven and allow to cool on a wire rack. When cool, use a table fork to pierce the circumference near the top and remove the tops. Leave the largest part of the puff on the bottom—remove just enough top to allow for spooning in the filling. If some of the dough has not completely puffed inside, remove it from the shell. Do not throw it away—mix it with any leftover cream filling and eat it; not pretty, but it's good tasting.

Fill the puffs with either sweetened whipped cream or with the Cream Filling recipe.

To dust the tops of the puffs with confectioners' sugar, put the sugar into a tea strainer and gently move a teaspoon back and forth in the strainer, directing the sugar onto the puffs. Serve.

Sour Cream Cake

½ cup cake flour
⅛ teaspoon baking soda
¼ cup unsalted butter or margarine
¼ cup sugar
1 tablespoon egg white
¼ cup sour cream
¼ to ½ teaspoon vanilla extract, or to taste

Preheat oven to 325° F.

Sift flour and baking soda together. Cream the butter and sugar, then add the egg white and sour cream. Mix in the flour, and beat well. Add the vanilla extract and stir. Pour into a greased 3½-inch by 2½-inch by 6-inch loaf pan. Bake for 35 to 40 minutes. Serve plain or frost as desired.

Angel Food Cake

This cake contains almost no cholesterol or sodium.

¼ cup egg white (about 2 egg whites)
¼ teaspoon cream of tartar
¼ cup granulated sugar, sifted 4 times
¼ cup cake flour, sifted 4 times with 1 tablespoon plus ½ teaspoon
   sugar
⅛ teaspoon vanilla extract
⅛ teaspoon lemon extract *or* lemon juice

Preheat oven to 300° F.

Beat egg white with cream of tartar until it forms soft peaks. Add the ¼ cup sifted sugar, folding small amounts at a time into the egg white. Sprinkle the sifted flour and sugar over the mixture. Gently fold into batter until all flour is moistened. Add vanilla and lemon extracts.

Pour batter into an ungreased individual 3¼-inch by 6-inch by 2-inch loaf pan or a small individual tube pan. Bake at 300° F. for 15 minutes, then increase oven heat to 375° and bake for 20 minutes more.

Pineapple Upside-Down Cake

$\frac{1}{2}$ tablespoon plus $1\frac{1}{2}$ teaspoons butter or margarine, divided
2 tablespoons sugar
$\frac{1}{4}$ egg·($\frac{3}{4}$ teaspoon yolk, $\frac{1}{2}$ tablespoon white)
$\frac{1}{4}$ cup flour, sifted
$\frac{3}{8}$ teaspoon baking powder
1 tablespoon plus 1 teaspoon milk
$\frac{1}{4}$ teaspoon vanilla extract
2 tablespoons brown sugar, firmly packed
$\frac{1}{2}$ can (8-ounce size) pineapple chunks, drained
4 Maraschino cherries, halved (optional)

Preheat oven to 375° F.

Cream sugar, egg, and $\frac{1}{2}$ tablespoon butter. Add sifted flour and baking powder, alternating with the milk. Beat well after each addition. Add the vanilla extract and mix well.

Melt the $1\frac{1}{2}$ teaspoons butter in a baking pan approximately 4 inches by 5 inches by 2 inches. Sprinkle the brown sugar over the melted butter, then arrange the pineapple and cherry halves on top. Pour in the cake batter gently and spread evenly. Bake for 25 to 30 minutes. The cake will be very light in color. When done, it should slightly resist the impression of a finger.

Save the pineapple juice for use in other recipes.

Favorite White Cake

6 tablespoons cake flour
$\frac{3}{8}$ teaspoon baking powder
1 tablespoon plus 1 teaspoon butter or margarine
4 tablespoons sugar
$\frac{1}{8}$ teaspoon vanilla extract
$1\frac{1}{8}$ teaspoons egg yolk
$\frac{1}{8}$ cup milk
1 tablespoon egg white, beaten stiff

Preheat oven to 350° F.

Sift flour and baking powder together. Cream butter until light and fluffy. Gradually add sugar, beating constantly until very fluffy. Beat in vanilla extract and egg yolk. (If you are doing this by hand, beat the egg yolk separately, then add to the cake mixture.) Gradually add the dry ingredients, alternating with the milk, and beating thoroughly after each addition. Carefully fold in the stiffly beaten egg white. Grease a foil pan about 4 inches by 5 inches by 2 inches, and line the bottom with wax paper. Pour in batter and bake about 25 minutes or until a toothpick comes out clean. The cake will be very light in color.

Excellent plain, or frost as desired.

Coconut Angel Food Cake

Make the recipe for Angel Food Cake (p. 183). Pour a little of the batter into the bottom of the pan until it is about $\frac{1}{2}$ inch deep. Spread a generous layer of shredded coconut (approximately $\frac{1}{4}$ cup) over the batter. Then add more batter, then coconut, and alternate layers of each, ending with batter on the top.

For an interesting effect, the coconut may be colored by adding a few drops of food coloring. Rub the coconut between your fingers until all shreds are colored.

Ice the cake with White Frosting (see recipe p. 188), to which a few drops of coconut flavoring may be added if desired.

Chocolate Cake Florence

Though not as feathery light as some cakes, this unusual cake is rich and satisfying, yet quite low in cholesterol and sodium and not too sweet. It is even better after it stands a day. And it stays moist and delectable for several days.

1 tablespoon butter or margarine
4 tablespoons sugar, divided
$1\frac{1}{2}$ teaspoons egg yolk
$4\frac{1}{2}$ teaspoons dry cocoa
$\frac{3}{4}$ teaspoon vegetable oil
$\frac{1}{4}$ teaspoon vanilla extract
$\frac{1}{4}$ cup cake flour
$\frac{1}{4}$ teaspoon baking powder
3 tablespoons milk
1 tablespoon egg white

Preheat oven to 325° F.

Cream butter and 3 tablespoons sugar. Add egg yolk and mix. Add cocoa, oil, and vanilla extract. Beat well. Combine flour and baking powder. Add one-third each of flour and milk to butter mixture; beat well. Add remainders of flour and milk in alternate stages, beating well after each addition.

In a separate bowl, using clean beater, beat the egg white until stiff, then fold in 1 tablespoon sugar. Fold beaten egg white into the cake batter.

Grease a 3½-inch by 6-inch by 2-inch loaf pan or equivalent-sized round pan. Line the bottom of the pan with wax paper cut to shape. Fill pan with batter about halfway full. Bake for 30 to 35 minutes. Do not overbake.

Cool. Slice cake in half lengthwise. Using Chocolate Frosting and Filling Florence (see below), spread the filling between the layers. Put filled layers together. Frost the sides and top of the cake.

Chocolate Frosting and Filling Florence

3 tablespoons plus 1 teaspoon cake flour
5 tablespoons milk, divided
2 tablespoons granulated sugar
4 teaspoons vegetable oil
2 tablespoons milk
Dash of salt, if desired
2 tablespoons dry cocoa
2 to 4 tablespoons confectioners' sugar

Mix flour and 3 tablespoons milk in a saucepan. Cook over low heat until it forms a thick, pasty mixture and leaves the sides of the pan. Set aside to cool thoroughly. Meanwhile, in a bowl mix together sugar, oil, 2 tablespoons milk, salt, and cocoa.

Cream this together, then add flour mixture. Beat again until smooth. If too thick, add more milk, a teaspoonful at a time, between beatings. Use part of this for the filling between the layers of cake.

To the remaining portion add 2 tablespoons confectioners' sugar. Beat well until it becomes a nice spreading consistency. If too thin, add more confectioners' sugar, 1 teaspoon at a time. After filling the cake and placing the 2 layers together, frost the sides and top of the cake.

This will fill and frost one 3½-inch by 6-inch by 2-inch cake.

White Frosting

3 tablespoons plus 1 teaspoon cake flour
5 tablespoons milk, divided
4 teaspoons vegetable oil
2 tablespoons granulated sugar
$\frac{1}{4}$ teaspoon vanilla extract
2 to 4 tablespoons confectioners' sugar

Mix the flour and 3 tablespoons milk in a saucepan. Cook over low heat until it forms a thick, pasty mixture and leaves the sides of the pan. Set aside to cool thoroughly.

Mix sugar, oil, 2 tablespoons milk, and vanilla extract. Add cooled flour mixture, and beat to a nice, thick consistency. If too thick, add a bit more milk, a teaspoonful at a time, between beatings. Part of this can be used for the filling between two layers of cake. Then add 2 tablespoons confectioners' sugar. Beat again until it forms a desired spreading consistency for frosting a cake. If it is too thin, add more confectioners' sugar, 1 teaspoon at a time.

Variations: Add $\frac{1}{4}$ teaspoon of another flavoring extract in addition to vanilla, but do this before adding any extra milk. Use lemon, orange, rum, banana, coconut, peppermint, or other flavoring. A few drops of food coloring corresponding to the flavoring may also be added. If using coffee, more confectioners' sugar will be needed. Cherries, chopped nuts, grated orange rind, or orange juice may also be used.

This frosting will remain soft, even when stored in a covered jar in the refrigerator.

This quantity will fill and frost 1 $3\frac{1}{2}$-inch by 6-inch by 2-inch loaf cake.

Fudge Almond Cake

$\frac{1}{8}$ pound ($\frac{1}{2}$ stick plus 2 tablespoons, or $\frac{1}{4}$ cup) butter or margarine, softened
$\frac{1}{3}$ cup plus $\frac{1}{2}$ tablespoon sugar, divided
6 tablespoons cocoa

3 tablespoons vegetable oil
1½ egg yolks (or 2 small yolks)
¼ teaspoon almond extract
1 tablespoon brewed coffee
1½ egg whites (or whites from 2 small eggs)
6 tablespoons sifted cake flour (or ¼ cup plus 2 tablespoons)

Preheat oven to 350° F.

Cream butter with ⅓ cup sugar until very pale and fluffy (about 5 minutes). Add cocoa and oil and continue beating. Add egg yolks, then almond extract, and coffee, mixing well until thoroughly blended.

Using clean beater, beat egg whites in a 2-cup measure or small bowl, until soft peaks form, then sprinkle in ½ tablespoon sugar and continue beating until stiff peaks form.

Add about a fourth of the egg whites to the batter and stir, then carefully fold in about a third of the remaining whites. When partially blended, sift in about a third of the flour, and fold into the batter. Alternate the remaining egg whites and flour until all is well blended. Do not beat, just carefully fold the mixture over and over. The batter will be thick.

Cut a piece of wax paper to fit bottom of 3-inch by 6-inch by 2-inch loaf pan, or a small round pan about 4 inches across—any baking dish that will hold about 2 cups of liquid. Grease sides of pan and put piece of wax paper in the bottom. Pour in batter. Bake about 20 minutes.

Cake will puff up in the center slightly but the edges will be firm. To test for doneness, pierce with a toothpick around the edges; the toothpick should come out clean and dry. (The center will leave an oily residue on the toothpick.) The center of the cake will be firm but soft, not like the edges in texture. This creamy-centered cake is rich and does not require an icing, unless you want one. If you plan to ice the cake, it must be thoroughly cool, so let it rest on a cake rack for an hour or so.

Orange Pound Cake

3 tablespoons butter or margarine
3 tablespoons sugar
1 small egg
6 tablespoons cake flour
¼ teaspoon baking powder
1½ to 2¼ teaspoons milk
¼ teaspoon vanilla extract
2 tablespoons grated orange rind
2 tablespoons jam or marmalade for filling cake, or to taste
Confectioners' sugar for dusting top of cake (optional)

Preheat oven to 350° F.

Cream the butter and sugar thoroughly, until light and fluffy. Beat the egg separately, until foamy, and add a bit at a time to the batter, beating well each time. If you are using an electric mixer, pour in the egg in a fine stream while the mixer beats the batter.

Sift the flour and baking powder together and fold into the batter, alternating with the milk and vanilla extract. Use only enough milk to make the batter drop easily from the spoon. Stir in orange rind.

Pour into greased individual loaf pan about 6 inches by 3 inches by 2 inches and bake approximately 40 to 45 minutes. Cake, when done, should spring back when lightly pressed with the fingertips, and sides will pull away from the pan slightly. Cool 5 minutes, then remove from the pan.

To fill the cake, split in half lengthwise. Spread one layer with jam or marmalade, replace the top and sprinkle with powdered sugar, or frost with your favorite frosting. If you use a white frosting (p. 188), add to it a few drops of orange flavoring or a few gratings of fresh orange peel.

Variation: Add 1 or 2 tablespoons chopped nuts or minced dried or candied fruits, dredged in a little flour, to the batter before baking.

Chocolate Malt Cake

7 tablespoons cake flour
$\frac{1}{2}$ teaspoon baking powder
3 tablespoons chocolate malt powder
1 tablespoon plus 1 teaspoon butter, margarine, or other shortening
$\frac{1}{4}$ cup sugar
$\frac{1}{2}$ large egg, or 1 small egg
$\frac{1}{8}$ cup (or 2 tablespoons) milk
$\frac{1}{4}$ teaspoon vanilla extract

Preheat oven to 350° F.

Sift the flour, baking powder, and malt powder together into a small bowl or onto a piece of wax paper.

Cream the butter and sugar until very light and fluffy. Add the egg and beat thoroughly. Add the dry ingredients, alternating with the milk, beating well after each addition. Add the vanilla extract. When all the batter is well blended, pour into a small loaf pan, 3 inches by 6 inches by $2\frac{1}{2}$ inches, or into a foil pan about 3 inches by 4 inches by 2 inches, or a round pan of approximately the same size.

Bake about 30 minutes, or until cake is golden on top and does not leave an impression when lightly touched with the tip of the finger.

Serve frosted or plain.

Quickie Cookies

1 cup flour
$\frac{1}{3}$ cup sugar
$\frac{1}{4}$ teaspoon baking powder
6 tablespoons butter or margarine
$\frac{1}{2}$ egg (1 tablespoon egg white and $1\frac{1}{2}$ teaspoons egg yolk)
$\frac{1}{2}$ teaspoon vanilla extract
6 to 8 tablespoons jam or preserves

Preheat oven to 350° F.

Mix all ingredients except jam to form a soft dough. Divide into two parts, about $\frac{3}{4}$ inch thick and 13 inches long. Place on ungreased cookie sheet, and make depressions about $\frac{1}{4}$ inch to $\frac{1}{2}$ inch deep with a knife handle, taking care you don't go too deep into the dough. Bake for 5 minutes. Remove the cookies from the oven, and fill the indentations with your favorite jam. Return filled cookies to the oven for 10 to 12 minutes, until delicately browned. Remove from oven. Immediately cut the cookies on the diagonal, using a sharp knife.

Rich Crispy Cookies

$\frac{1}{4}$ pound unsalted butter or margarine, softened
$\frac{1}{4}$ cup sugar
$\frac{3}{4}$ teaspoon vanilla extract
$\frac{3}{4}$ teaspoon almond extract
$\frac{3}{4}$ cup flour

Preheat oven to 350° F.

Cream butter and sugar with the vanilla and almond extracts until light and fluffy. Sift in flour, a little at a time, beating well after each addition.

There are two ways you can bake these cookies:

1. Scoop the dough onto the center of a large, ungreased baking sheet. Shape the dough into a square a scant $\frac{1}{2}$ inch thick. Bake in the middle of the oven for about 35 minutes or until it is firm to the touch and the top is golden brown. The square will spread. Remove from oven and immediately cut into $1\frac{1}{2}$-inch squares. Place cookies on a wire rack to cool.

2. Drop spoonfuls of dough, about the size of a small walnut, on a large, ungreased baking sheet, 1 inch apart. Bake for 15 minutes, until golden brown. Remove from oven and place cookies on a wire rack to cool. Makes about 20 cookies 1 to $1\frac{1}{2}$ inches in diameter.

These cookies keep well for 2 to 3 weeks if stored in a tightly covered container.

Variations: Divide the dough into thirds. Use one third to make plain Rich Crispy Cookies. To another third of the dough, add a few drops of yellow food coloring and $\frac{1}{4}$ teaspoon lemon extract *or* 1 teaspoon grated lemon peel. To the remaining third of the dough, add $1\frac{1}{2}$ tablespoons of cocoa and 1 to 2 tablespoons ground nuts, then mix thoroughly. Bake as directed in a preheated 350° F. oven. The result: three varieties of rich, crispy cookies!

Meringue Cookies

2 egg whites at room temperature
1 cup granulated sugar
½ teaspoon vanilla extract, crème de menthe, or other flavoring
Flour

Preheat oven to 250° F.

Beat egg whites until foamy. Slowly add the sugar, a bit at a time, continuing to beat until the egg whites are very stiff—at least 5 minutes, with electric beater. Add vanilla extract or desired flavoring.

Grease a cookie sheet with butter or margarine, sprinkle lightly with flour, and shake to cover it evenly. Tap off all excess flour.

Drop the mixture by spoonfuls onto the cookie sheet. These can be large (2 inches high and 1 inch across) or smaller, like a small drop cookie. Or put the mixture into a pastry tube, using a large star tip, or shape it into rosettes. The shape and size will not change during the baking.

Place in the middle of the oven and bake for about 50 minutes if large size, about 30 minutes if small. Cookies should remain colorless. If they begin to take on color, lower the oven heat to about 200° F. When done, cookies will be dry and crisp, but tender.

These are especially good cookies for those on low-cholesterol diets.

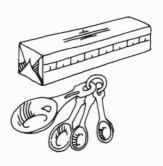

Grandma Crawford's Sugar Cookies

Yield: 12 to 15 cookies

2 tablespoons butter, margarine, or shortening
¼ cup sugar
½ egg (1½ teaspoons yolk, 1½ tablespoons white)
¾ teaspoon cream or milk
¼ teaspoon vanilla extract
½ teaspoon baking powder
½ cup flour (approximately)

Preheat oven to 375° F.

Beat butter, sugar, egg, milk, and vanilla extract until very light colored, about 5 or 6 minutes with an electric beater. (If you are doing this by hand, cream the butter and sugar, beat the egg separately, then add to creamed mixture and beat again. Add the milk and mix thoroughly.)

Combine baking powder with flour and sift part of it into creamed mixture. Beat well. Add remaining flour mixture; continue beating until all flour is mixed in. Dough should be soft and smooth and easy to handle. If it is still fairly sticky, add a bit more flour, about a teaspoonful at a time, until the dough can be easily handled.

Chill for about an hour, or place in freezer for 15 to 20 minutes.

Roll dough on a floured board with a floured rolling pin (or bottle) to about ¼ inch thick. Cut with cookie cutter or drinking glass dipped in flour. Place cookies on ungreased cookie sheet about 1 inch apart, and sprinkle with granulated sugar. Bake for about 8 minutes.

Grandma Snyder's Sour Cream Sugar Cookies

$\frac{1}{4}$ cup butter, margarine, or shortening
$\frac{1}{4}$ cup sugar
$\frac{1}{4}$ cup commercial sour cream
1 cup sifted regular flour (approximately)
$\frac{1}{4}$ teaspoon baking soda
$\frac{1}{4}$ teaspoon baking powder
$\frac{1}{2}$ to 1 teaspoon vanilla extract

Preheat oven to 350° F.

Beat butter and sugar until creamy and light colored. Add the sour cream and mix well. Sift and measure the flour and add the baking soda and baking powder to the flour. Sift about half the flour mixture into the butter mixture and mix well. Add the vanilla extract and mix again. Add remaining flour and mix until all traces of flour are gone.

Dough should be soft, smooth, and easy to handle. Chill for about an hour, or place in freezer for about 20 minutes.

Roll dough a little less than $\frac{3}{8}$ inch thick on a floured board with a floured rolling pin or long bottle. Cut with a cookie cutter or drinking glass dipped in flour. Gather remaining dough pieces and reroll, cut more cookies; continue until all dough is used. Sprinkle granulated sugar over the tops.

Place on ungreased cookie sheet, leaving about 1 inch between them. Bake for about 8 minutes, or until very lightly browned.

Makes about 20 cookies $2\frac{1}{4}$ inches across.

Old-Fashioned Strawberry Shortcake

Prepare the sauce while the cake is baking.

Ingredients	For one piece 2½" x 2½" x 2" (dessert size)	For a cake 5" x 5" x 2" (dinner size)
Butter or margarine	2 teaspoons	1 tablespoon and 1 teaspoon
Flour	¼ cup and ¾ teaspoon	½ cup and 1½ teaspoons
Baking powder	⅓ teaspoon	⅔ teaspoon
Sugar	¾ teaspoon	1½ teaspoons
Milk	4 teaspoons	2 tablespoons and 2 teaspoons

Preheat oven to 375° F.

Place butter in a small bowl. Sift in flour and baking powder. Add sugar. Mix until crumbly, using a table fork. Add milk and stir together to form a small, soft ball.

At this point, you can do one of two things: Place the dough into a very lightly oiled baking pan, and pat it out even; or divide dough in half and place 1 piece in the pan, patting it flat. Butter that piece, then put the remaining piece on top, and pat it flat.

Bake until browned, about 20 to 25 minutes. Separate the two halves, or cut the cake in half through the center horizontally. Spoon some of the sauce over bottom half, then place the top on it, and spoon the rest of the sauce over the top. Serve immediately, or let cool.

Strawberry Sauce for Shortcake

Double the following quantities for the 5-inch by 5-inch by 2-inch cake.

½ pint strawberries
¾ teaspoon sugar
½ tablespoon water (optional)

Wash berries by soaking them a few minutes, then swish them around to loosen any sand that still may be attached. Remove stems. Then mash them into small pieces, using a glass. (You can slice them with a knife if you prefer.) Sprinkle the sugar over them. Add the water if you like a lot of juice to soak into the cake. (You can add even more water if you wish.)

Let berries stand at room temperature, stirring occasionally, while shortcake is baking.

Peach Sauce for Shortcake

Substitute peaches for strawberries in above recipe. Use 1 large peach for dessert-size cake, 2 or more for dinner size. If smaller peaches are used, you will need at least 1 cup sliced peaches.

Peel and slice peaches thin, then cut slices in half crosswise. Sprinkle with sugar and add water, as above.

You may also use 1 cup (or more, as desired) of any other juicy fruit, such as blueberries, raspberries, or blackberries.

Chocolate Pudding

1 tablespoon flour
2 tablespoons cocoa (or ½ square unsweetened chocolate, grated)
¼ cup sugar
½ cup milk
¾ teaspoon butter or margarine
1 egg yolk
¾ teaspoon vanilla extract

Mix flour, cocoa (or chocolate), and sugar together in a 1-quart sauce-pan, or a double boiler if available. Pour in a little milk and stir until all dry ingredients are moistened and blended in.

Gradually add the rest of the milk, stirring to blend. Add the butter and stir well. Set pan over boiling water or over low to medium heat and stir constantly with a wire whisk or spoon until pudding is smooth and thick. Take care not to let it burn.

When thick, remove from heat and add the egg yolk, stirring to blend well with the chocolate mixture. Return the pan to heat and cook a minute or so longer to cook the egg, stirring constantly. Remove from heat and add the vanilla extract. Stir. Pour into pudding or sherbet dish and cool. Makes ¾ cup of pudding.

To Make Chocolate Pie

Preheat oven to 350° F.

Pour mixture into prebaked tart shell. Using clean beater, beat 1 egg white until it forms stiff peaks. Blend in 1 to 2 teaspoons of sugar as the whites foam. Spoon the meringue over the chocolate and bake until meringue browns lightly at the tips.

Grandma's Vanilla Pudding

3 teaspoons cornstarch
4 teaspoons granulated sugar
$\frac{1}{2}$ cup milk
$\frac{1}{2}$ teaspoon butter or margarine
$\frac{1}{4}$ teaspoon vanilla extract

Mix the cornstarch and sugar in a 1-quart saucepan or in the top of a double boiler. Add a little milk and mix until smooth. Slowly add remaining milk and butter and stir well. Cook over low to medium heat on an asbestos pad or over boiling water. Stir constantly and watch carefully because this will burn easily.

When thick and smooth, remove from heat and stir in the vanilla extract. Serve in sherbet dish warm or chilled.

Variations: Garnish with crushed or sliced fruits, such as peaches, bananas, or berries.

Makes about $\frac{3}{4}$ cup.

Glossary

Bake To cook by dry heat. Also known as "roast" when applied to meat. One usually "roasts" beef, pork, lamb, and chicken, but "bakes" a ham, cake, cookies. The method is the same and usually is done in an oven at a specified temperature.

Barbecue To cook meat or other food on a grate over an open fire. Also refers to meat that has been marinated in a highly seasoned oil-and-vinegar sauce and then broiled. Also, a portable firepit over which food is cooked.

Baste To moisten meat during roasting (or baking) with melted butter, pan drippings, wine, marinade, or other liquid by spooning it over meat or by using a baster (a long-handled tube with a bulb at the end—like a giant-sized eyedropper).

Batter A mixture of flour, liquid, and other ingredients thin enough to pour or drop from a spoon or of a consistency to adhere to meat, vegetables, or fruits. Food may be dipped in a batter before frying.

Beat A rapid over-and-over motion with a spoon, fork, or whisk to blend ingredients in a mixture or to break down lumps. A hand eggbeater or an electric mixer may also be used.

Blanch To cook in boiling water from 3 to 5 minutes in order to lighten the color of a food, loosen skins, to cause food to shrink in volume, to precook for a very short period of time, or to stop enzymatic action before freezing or canning.

Blend To stir gently just enough to mix the ingredients.

Boil To heat liquid until full of bubbles (212° F.). A "rolling boil" is one that cannot be stirred down—the moving of a large spoon in it will not diminish the bubbles.

Boil down To boil the liquid until it has partially reduced in quantity (by the process of evaporation).

Bone To cut meat in order to remove the bone or bones before cooking.

Braise To cook slowly in a little fat (such as butter or oil) and a little liquid in a covered pan.

Bread To coat with fine bread or cracker crumbs, or sometimes crushed corn flakes. Food to be breaded is dipped in a liquid or semiliquid, such as beaten egg or milk, and then into crumbs before frying.

Broil To cook by direct exposure to open heat, such as electric coils, gas flame, or charcoal, with or without a pan, on a rack that allows fat to drip down away from the meat. Heating elements may be above the meat or below.

Broiler The equipment used to broil meat as described above. Also refers to a young chicken up to about $2\frac{1}{2}$ pounds dressed weight, tender enough to cook by broiling.

Brown To cook over high heat until food becomes light to medium brown in color. Usually a small amount of fat is used.

Chop To cut into small pieces, not necessarily uniform in size. Pieces can be anywhere from $\frac{1}{4}$ to $\frac{3}{4}$ inch in size, but thicknesses should be even.

Clarify To separate the solids from the liquid butter. Place butter in pan and heat over low heat until the solids separate. The clear liquid is then carefully drained off and used for such purposes as a dip for cooked shrimp or lobster.

Coat To cover or cling to an item evenly. When sauce is thick enough to coat a spoon, it clings to spoon and will not run off. Food such as meat or salad greens may be coated with flour or salad dressing, respectively tossing and turning it until all pieces are lightly and evenly covered.

Cream To beat or blend elements together to the consistency of very thick cream, such as beating butter and sugar together until smooth and thick and a lighter color than the butter was originally.

Cube To cut into medium-sized pieces, about $\frac{1}{2}$ to 1 inch square, as with meat or vegetables.

Cut in To blend elements until crumbly. Use two table knives or a pastry blender in short cutting motions to blend flour and butter or other shortening.

Dash A very small amount, usually less than a pinch. To add a dash of spice or salt from a shaker container, a quick flip of the wrist (like an exclamation point) will release enough spice from the container.

Deep-fry To cook in a large quantity of hot fat or oil until food is browned and cooked through and has a crisp exterior. High heat is usually used, and food must be covered by the oil.

Dice To cut into small cubes about $\frac{1}{8}$ to $\frac{1}{4}$ inch square, usually done to vegetables.

Dissolve To blend a solid element such as yeast or cornstarch into liquid until it melts or disappears.

Drain To remove liquid from pan, jar, or other container. Usually accomplished by pouring contents of pan into a colander or sieve or holding cover against container, leaving a very small opening so liquid can run off while contents remain in container.

Dredge To coat food with flour, cornstarch, or bread crumbs. The flour or other coating is placed in a bowl; solid food, such as meat, is then added and tossed until coated. The food may also be placed in a bag and shaken to coat the solid pieces. Nuts and dried fruits must be dredged to prevent them from sinking to the bottom of the pan while cooking in a cake.

Dribble To sprinkle in small trickling stream or flow. Sugar or nuts may be dribbled over the top of a cake so that the pieces fall in a hit-and-miss pattern.

Drippings Fat or juices drawn from meat during cooking.

Drop To drop by spoonfuls is to let fall or ease off a spoon in one mass, in one place. Also, the smallest practical unit of liquid measure. Twenty drops equal 1 teaspoon.

Fold To incorporate a food ingredient into a mixture by repeated gentle overturning—all in the same direction—without stirring or beating. Used especially to incorporate beaten egg whites into a batter.

French-cut To cut in thin lengthwise strips before cooking, as with string beans or potatoes.

Fry To cook in a pan or on a griddle over heat, especially with the use of fat, such as butter or oil. *See also* Deep-fry.

Garnish To add decorative or savory touches to food, such as to an open-face sandwich or a dish or tray of food. Typical garnishes are watercress, whole or chopped parsley, whole crabapples, chopped nuts, and chopped hard-boiled egg.

Glaze A liquid preparation applied to food on which it hardens or forms a firm glossy coating, as in a glazed doughnut or glazed ham. A glaze often contains sugar.

Grate To pulverize or shred very fine by rubbing against a grater.

Grease To rub a pan with a fat such as butter or oil to keep food from sticking to the pan while cooking.

Handful As much as or as many as the hand will grasp.

Knead To mix and stretch, as dough, until pliable and elastic. Press dough down and outward with the heel of the hand; fold in half, turn one-quarter turn, and press down again. Repeat usually for at least 10 minutes.

Marinate To soak meat or fish in a sauce usually made of oil, vinegar, and spices, which enhances the flavor and tenderizes the meat. The sauce is called a marinade and may also contain wine or other liquids.

Mince To cut in very fine pieces.

Parboil To boil briefly, as with vegetables to barely soften them, usually not more than 3 to 5 minutes.

Poach To cook in liquid, such as with eggs or fish.

Pot roast A less tender cut of meat cooked slowly in a covered pot with liquid and sometimes seasonings and vegetables. The long cooking in liquid tenderizes the meat.

Reconstitute To stir gently until liquid and solids are evenly distributed and no traces of solids remain.

Reduce To boil down partially, according to requirements of the recipe.

Roast To cook by dry heat, usually beef or chicken. The method is the same as baking, and is done in an oven at a specified temperature.

Sauté To fry quickly, stirring the food or shaking the pan. Sautéed onions are cooked in a small amount of butter or oil over a moderate heat, shaking the pan so the onions do not burn.

Scald To heat milk slowly until a film forms over the top, but the milk does not simmer at the edges or come to a boil. Scalding is to cook at a temperature just below boiling. When scalding milk, remove and discard the thick film before using in a recipe.

Score To make shallow cuts across the surface or edge of a food such as meat. Sometimes called "marking." To "score" the edges of a steak to keep it from curling, gashes are cut every inch or so, from the outside of the fat, through the little layer of gristle and just barely into the meat, all the way around the fat, so the meat will stay flat while cooking.

Sift To pass dry ingredients, such as flour or sugar, through a fine sieve (called a sifter). The purpose is to break down any lumps into fine powdery particles. Flour is also sifted to add air into it before cooking.

Simmer To boil lightly. Little bubbles may form around the edge of the pan and sometimes over the surface, but there should not be any large, rapidly boiling bubbles. Simmering is done over a very low flame. Vegetable soup is simmered for a long period of time, over a low heat, so liquid just barely moves around the edges.

Steam To cook by the heat of steam rising from boiling water. Food is placed in a container, such as a metal basket or foil packet; the container is then placed in water (for the packet) or over the water (for the basket). As the steam rises, it cooks the food.

Whip To beat vigorously, as in whipping cream or egg whites. The more vigorously the liquid is whipped, the more air enters the liquid and causes it to expand. Usually done with the highest setting on an electric mixer. A hand-held whisk or eggbeater may also be used.

Index